CHELSEA

1 Unloading barges at Lindsey Jetty
From the painting by Walter Greaves

CHELSEA

William Gaunt

London
B. T. BATSFORD LTD

First Published, 1954

Made and Printed in Great Britain by Jarrold and Sons Ltd.
London and Norwich for the Publishers
B. T. BATSFORD LTD.
4, Fitzhardinge Street, London, W.1

PREFACE

THE written history of Chelsea is rich in detail, both topographical and personal, whether one considers the many books of which it is the main theme, the biographies of its notable residents, or the references to it in letters, diaries, novels, essays and poems.

Of general surveys, the earliest date back to the beginning of the eighteenth century. The first to be published was that of John Bowack, a writing master at Westminster School, and was included in his larger project *The Antiquities of Middlesex* (1706). To that extent Bowack may be looked on as the first Chelsea historian, though some years earlier, *c.* 1700, an account of the parish, especially useful as regards the ownership and division of land, was compiled in manuscript by Dr. John King, the "antiquarian rector of Chelsea" and his MS. and accompanying maps, preserved in the Chelsea Public Library, remain a valuable source of topographical knowledge.

Chelsea also has its place, topographically, in the principal work of the Rev. Daniel Lysons, *The Environs of London* (1792-6); but its classic history, in which architectural and human interest are combined, is, of course, Thomas Faulkner's *An Historical and Topographical Description of Chelsea and Its Environs* "interspersed", so the sub-title of the 1829 edition reads, "with biographical anecdotes of illustrious and eminent persons who have resided in Chelsea during the three preceding centuries". Its copiousness set a standard, though later histories, with more exact knowledge and no less enthusiasm have surpassed it. The most fruitful period of historical study may be roughly dated between 1880 and 1914. In the *Village of Palaces*, the Rev. A. G. L'Estrange gave (1880) an entertaining picture of the past; in *Memorials of Old Chelsea*, Alfred Beaver amassed (1892) an astonishing quantity of information on old and (then) recent history. The main honours must, however, be divided between Reginald Blunt, for whom every name and landmark was full of storied life, and Randall Davies who combined the scientific spirit of exact enquiry with a connoisseur's appreciation. Reginald Blunt has given us a whole series of delightful studies, *The Carlyles' Chelsea Home* (1895), *Paradise Row* (1906), *In Cheyne Walk and Thereabouts* (1914)—not to speak of his serviceable *Handbook to Chelsea* (1900). In his *Chelsea Old Church* (1904), Randall Davies produced a work of authority, not only on the church and its monuments, but on the old families of Chelsea, their possessions and connections (a strangely interesting web of local relationship). The final, monumental record of architecture (pre-nineteenth-century) is contained in the four volumes in the Survey of London devoted to Chelsea (1909-27), the Parish of Chelsea I and II, The Old Church III and the Royal Hospital IV. To this Dr. Nikolaus Pevsner's *London* (excluding the City of Westminster) in The Buildings of

England series (1952) is complementary, its section on Chelsea not only compressing a great deal into comparatively small space but continuing the record of architectural style to the present day.

Particular aspects of Chelsea are further described in: *A Memoir of the Botanic Garden at Chelsea* by Henry Field, continued by R. H. Semple (1878), which sets out Chelsea's contribution to the study and use of herbs and medicinal plants; *The London Pleasure Gardens of the 18th Century* by W. and A. E. Wroth (1896), which fully describes Ranelagh; the Survey of London Committee's monograph (1908) on Crosby Place; the *Cheyne Book of Chelsea China and Pottery* (1924) edited by Reginald Blunt; while the annual reports of the Chelsea Society, founded in 1927, are unfailingly of interest in their chronicle of preservation and change and Chelsea studies in general.

In its biographical aspect, the record of Chelsea begins splendidly with the description by Erasmus of the character and household of Sir Thomas More and the biography of the famous man compiled by his son-in-law, William Roper (1496–1578), who married More's daughter Margaret in 1525 and wrote with the authority of at least ten years' intimacy, partly domestic and partly in legal collaboration with Sir Thomas.

"The two hundred years that have elapsed since Hans Sloane's death have dimmed the outline of his figure to such an extent that for many people he is nothing but a street and a square" remarks Sir Gavin de Beer, Director of the British Museum (Natural History), but he has done much to remedy this with his scholarly life, *Sir Hans Sloane and the British Museum* (1953). Opposite of dim figures and subject of a vast number of books, Thomas and Jane Welsh Carlyle can be pictured in Chelsea by means of the several collections of their letters, Thomas Carlyle's *Reminiscences*, the *History of His Life in London, 1834–1881* by James Anthony Froude, and, among many other works, the *Life of Carlyle* by David A. Wilson and *Necessary Evil—The Life of Jane Welsh Carlyle* by Lawrence and Elizabeth Hanson.

The biographies of Turner, by Walter Thornbury (to be regarded with caution) and A. J. Finberg, as a serious authority, may be compared for their account of Turner's Chelsea period. Thomas Balston's *Life of John Martin* has much relevant Chelsea detail. *Recollections of D. G. Rossetti and his Circle* by Treffry Dunn and *Recollections of Dante Gabriel Rossetti* by T. Hall Caine illuminate his life at Cheyne Walk. Whistler can be followed through Chelsea in the life by Joseph and Elizabeth Robins Pennell, their *Whistler Journal* and in the life by James Laver. For a description of the Chelsea setting, mood and circle of Rossetti and Whistler the present writer would also refer to his *The Pre-Raphaelite Tragedy* and *The Aesthetic Adventure*.

Among other relevant biographies are those of Count Zinzendorf by the Rev. A. G. Spangenberg, of the De Morgans by A. M. W. Sterling, of Charles Keene by G. S. Layard, of J. S. Sargent by Evan Charteris, of Wilson Steer by D. S. McColl, of Charles Conder by John Rothenstein.

PREFACE

The chapter on Chelsea in the 'nineties in *Men and Memories* by Sir William Rothenstein gives interesting glimpses of its artists at that time.

Incidental references to Chelsea in English letters are numerous enough to make a delightful anthology. Such are to be found in the diaries of John Evelyn and Samuel Pepys, in Swift's *Journal to Stella*, in Defoe's *Tour through England and Wales*, in *The Tatler*, in Gay's *Trivia*, in the novels of Fielding and Smollett, the letters of Horace Walpole, the autobiography of Leigh Hunt, the commentaries of both the Carlyles, *The Gentle Art of Making Enemies*, the letters of Henry James.

The author has gratefully made use of the extensive and varied material in the present attempt to describe the development of Chelsea as, so to speak, a "living organism".

He is indebted to Mr. Basil Marsden Smedley, O.B.E., Secretary of the Chelsea Society, for his helpful interest and for his aid in tracking down the first reference to Dr. Johnson's supposed experiments in firing porcelain in Chelsea, and also to Mr. and Mrs. Marsden Smedley for reading the proofs and their most valuable comments; to Captain C. T. G. Dean, M.B.E., author of *The Royal Hospital, Chelsea*, whose specialist knowledge has been of great help on many points; and to Mr. William King of the British Museum for looking through and making suggestions on the passages referring to Chelsea Porcelain. He is also indebted to the Chelsea Arts Club for access to unpublished letters, reminiscences and notes relating to the origin and early days of the Club; to the courtesy of the Librarian of the Chelsea Public Library in being permitted to examine its large collection of pictorial documents, to the Borough Librarian of Wandsworth for information regarding the paintings by Walter Greaves at the old Streatham Town Hall, and to the Streatham Engineering Company for permission to see them. He gratefully acknowledges also the most helpful services of the London Library and the continued assistance and valuable suggestions given by Mr. Samuel Carr of Messrs. B. T. Batsford during the preparation of the work.

London, 1954   *William Gaunt*

ACKNOWLEDGMENT

FOR permission to reproduce illustrations the Author and Publishers would like to thank:

The Addison Gallery of American Art, Philips Academy, Andover, U.S.A., for Fig. 43; Basel: the Oeffentliche Kunstsammlung, for Fig. 3; Sir Max Beerbohm, for Fig. 37; The British Museum, and the Avalon Press, for Fig. 16; Chelsea Public Library: the Borough Librarian and the Library Committee, for Figs. 8, 14, 15, 20, 21, 30, 31, 44, 47 and 48; The Gernsheim Collection, for Fig. 38; A. F. Kersting, F.R.P.S., for Figs. 9, 10, 22–5, 34, 35, 49 and 50; The Leicester Galleries, London, for Fig. 46; The National Buildings Record, for Fig. 14; The National Gallery, for Fig. 19; The National Portrait Gallery, for Figs. 26–8 and 39–42; Picture Post Library, for Figs. 32 and 33; The Royal Commission on Historical Monuments, for Fig. 7; The Scottish National Portrait Gallery, for Fig. 29; The late Will F. Taylor, for Fig. 5; The Victoria and Albert Museum, for Figs. 36 and 45; The remainder of the illustrations are from the Publishers' own Collection.

Figure 7 is Crown Copyright and is reproduced by permission of the Controller of Her Majesty's Stationery Office.

CONTENTS

THE ILLUSTRATIONS

IN THE TEXT

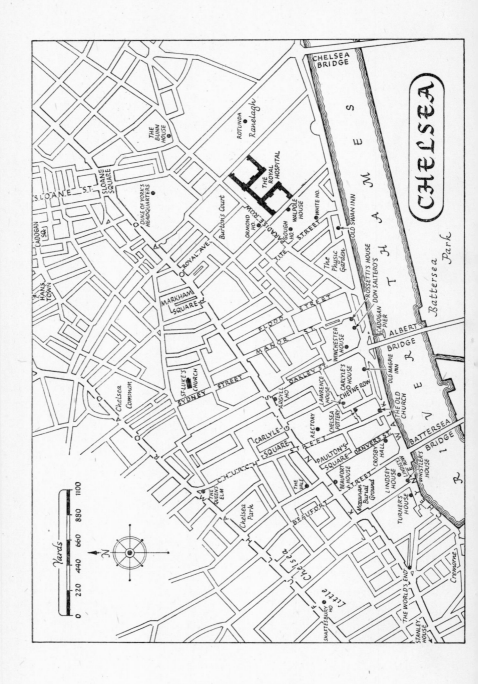

I

THE VILLAGE AND THE MANOR

OF the many villages that London has absorbed, and to some extent preserved, within its extending framework, Chelsea is perhaps the most remarkable for strong local traditions and associations that have quite surprisingly outlasted or accompanied material change.

It has been so intimately linked with the lives of a number of famous people that one might say its story is theirs—the story of Sir Thomas More, Sir Hans Sloane, Thomas Carlyle, Dante Gabriel Rossetti, James McNeill Whistler. . . . The personal legend, in this comparatively self-contained "village", has been more powerful than elsewhere in London; painters and writers who have lived in other districts, here seem more distinctly and definitely at home. The great Turner, mysterious in his Queen Anne Street mansion, ceases to be remote when he comes to Chelsea: exists for us vividly as a character of the neighbourhood. To understand his celebrated seclusion in Cheyne Walk one needs only to visit the delightful cottage in which he lodged (very trim in these days with its well-cared-for brick and its lemon-coloured door): one can almost see him on the roof with its balcony, that commands such an excellent view of the river in its chromatic mist.

Or Rossetti—there was a man of many addresses, interesting always wherever he happened to be, yet more easily separable from Red Lion Square or Blackfriars than from Queens House, 16 Cheyne Walk, the stronghold of his mature years. Even the student of architecture will be compelled to think of the tenant as well as the architect of certain notable houses. It is true enough to say that the present No. 24 Cheyne Row, built by Lord Cheyne in 1708, is a good specimen of the Queen Anne domestic style; yet it is intensely permeated by the personalities of its nineteenth-century occupants, Thomas and Jane Welsh Carlyle; and the pilgrim goes to the first floor drawing-room less to study a period interior than to stand where *The French Revolution* was written and to experience what-ever may linger of the mental atmosphere of an extraordinary household.

"Carlyle Studios", "Rossetti Mansions"—Chelsea conserves its associations in several forms: a Chelsea chemist has even advertised the "Carlyle Bouquet", the description, "though powerful, it is not heavy, for the odour is as refreshing as that brought by a summer breeze from a garden full of bloom", accompanied by a wood-engraving of the great man. Tradition is persistent in other ways. The variants on its late seventeenth-and early eighteenth-century architecture, though not exclusive to Chelsea, are so much in evidence there as almost to constitute a local revival. "Chelsea Arts"—the words go naturally together, and applied to modern institutions continually remind us that it has long been, and still is, a chief resort of artists in general. "Chelsea" figurines are still made by artist-craftsmen though the original porcelain manufactory ceased to operate in Lawrence Street about the year 1768. The Chelsea Flower Show per-petuates the historic celebrity of its gardens, already established in the days of Evelyn and Pepys.

The search for the historical origins of this well-defined place-personality need go no further back than the sixteenth century: though one may dubiously and briefly refer to specula-tions as to its ancient existence and name. The historian of London, Maitland, argued that Chelsea was the point at which Julius Caesar forded the Thames in pursuit of the retreating Britons. Greatly to his satisfaction Maitland discovered a ford, in the year 1738, "about ninety feet west of the south-west angle of Chelsea College Gardens", which at least suggests that the theory was tenable. The name indicates a settlement of Anglo-Saxons, though in its numerous early spellings it is one of the mysterious grotesques of etymology—Chelchaya, Cealchyde, Cealchythe, Cealchyll, Cercehede. . . . What are we to make of its thirty different spellings? Possibly it was a "Chesil-sey", or shelf of sand by the water, to be compared with the Chesil Bank outside Weymouth Harbour or Selsey on the Sussex

2 A late eighteenth-century view of Chelsea seen across the river from Battersea Churchyard

From a contemporary print

3 Sir Thomas More and his family, about 1528

From the study by Hans Holbein

Coast: kindred with its neighbour across the Thames, Battersea —Peters ey or Patricks ey, piece of land near water belonging to the Abbey of St. Peter at Westminster. On the other hand, the persistent "d" or "th" of the termination, may signify "hythe" or wharf as in the reference to a synod at "Cealchythe" in the Anglo Saxon Chronicle, A.D. 785. Assuming (which is not beyond all doubt) that Cealchythe was Chelsea, it may well have been a "chalk wharf", not because it is a district of chalk but because chalk may have been landed there—and was certainly a material used in the older parts of the old church. But for all practical purposes it seems enough to remark that the simplified form, Chelsey, was in use in Tudor times and that Dean Swift, referring to his sojourn in "Church Lane", already spells Chelsea in the modern way.

In the roughly triangular figure of the metropolitan borough on the modern map of London; with its base on the Thames, between Chelsea Bridge and the industrial terminus of Lots Road, its apex at Knightsbridge; the ancient manorial plan can be discerned. Towards the western end of the river frontage was the village nucleus of small houses clustering near the church. Tributary streams bounded it on either side. A creek flowing from Wormwood Scrubbs into the Thames defined its western corner. To the east the meanderings of the West Bourne can be traced in the boundary that zigzags its way through the streets on the eastern side of Sloane Street. The opposite and more regular side of the triangle follows the course of the old road to the next riverside village of Fulham. Fields, park and common land filled in the area into which London in the nineteenth century was to pour its buildings and increasing population. As a pleasant rural spot, not too far from London by road or river, Chelsea emerges from obscurity with the advent of Sir Thomas More who built his house there about the year 1520 and became the first of the famous residents whose affection for it may be called a creative influence on its history.

Sir Thomas More was not a country gentleman or lord of the manor in any except a cultural sense (though sharing the manorial privilege of a chapel in Chelsea Church) but the prototype of

Londoner seeking retreat. Born in Milk Street, sent to school at St. Anthony's, Threadneedle Street, trained in the law in the Inns of Court, drawn somewhat reluctantly into a political career, he had, save for his years at Oxford and until middle-age, spent most of his life in the city. When he came to Chelsea he was a man of forty or a little more, Master of Requests and high in favour with King Henry VIII, the friend of the great scholars of his time and author of that classic, sociological romance, *Utopia*, precursor of many ideal "nowheres".

Utopia, it has been acutely remarked "was but the author's home writ large" (Maurice Adams). There was a delightful view across the river of the woods and pastures on the Surrey side. Waterfowl flew among the reeds and where now the chimneys of industrial undertakings smoke. The pure waters of the Thames teemed with fish: salmon, trout, pike, carp, roach, dace, perch, chub, barbel, eels, lampreys, flounders, gudgeon. No doubt they fished then, opposite the church, in six or seven feet of water (as Thomas Faulkner, historian of Chelsea, was later to advise). The peace and quiet of the country enfolded the area of what is now the King's Road, to which the gardens of More's house extended.

For several reasons his life in these Utopian surroundings remains curiously vivid. His own personality so distinct, though subtle enough to be inconsistent and in some respects, to the modern mind, puzzling, moved those who knew him to make the intimate records that have been often quoted. Holbein has made him and his domestic circle in the Chelsea house visible to us. Finally, his execution throws its own lurid gleam on the idyllic retirement he stoically gave up. Nothing remains of Tudor Chelsea save a few mellow fragments of brick wall. We must in imagination reconstruct the house that Erasmus described, at second hand, as "not mean nor invidiously grand but comfortable" and the Jesuit, Ellis Heywood (in estate-agent terms) as a "beautiful and commodious residence". Imagination is supported by the excellent view of Beaufort House drawn by Leonard Knyff and engraved by Kip, dated 1699(6). It is now generally accepted that Beaufort House stood on the site

Beaufort House

of More's, Kip's print representing the mansion as rebuilt by Sir Robert Cecil, afterwards Lord Salisbury, who took possession in 1597.

The original house, then, stood where Beaufort Street was later built: and set back some distance from the river: being approached by two garden courts, the inner, guarded by two gate-houses. It is to be assumed they had flat roofs from which More enjoyed the view. One of them was the scene of his adventure with a lunatic who threatened to throw him over and was baffled by More who threw a little dog to the ground and persuaded the lunatic to go down after it, meanwhile bolting the door and calling for help. At the tree-lined river-front was a quay where More's barge waited to take him to the offices of state business at Westminster. Behind the house stretched the gardens where the guests, as Heywood relates, surveyed "almost all the noble city of London" from a green hillock and admired the "lovely flowers and sprays of fruit trees, admirably placed and interwoven"—less formal in arrangement, the description suggests, than in 1696.

Two plans, found by Mr. Walter H. Godfrey in the Salisbury archives, and described in the L.C.C. Survey of London (Chelsea: Part II) seem to represent the original ground and first floor before the rebuilding: from which we visualise the

Tudor porch flanked by projecting bays, and note the little chapel with a room above, having an open floor, so that those in it could share in the service. The inner stair near it led to a door opening on a long eastern terrace, appearing also in Kip's view but probably built by More.

It was on this property that he spent some fourteen years, until his attainder in 1535: returning home with relief, from the public life that led him to the uncomfortable eminence of Lord Chancellor. All chroniclers agree that the Chelsea household, depicted from the life by Holbein in a celebrated drawing(3), was a happy one. We see Sir Thomas with his father, Sir John More, at left, Alice, his second wife, with a pet monkey beside her, in front of her, Margaret Roper and Cecily Heron, his eldest and youngest daughters, to his right, the second daughter, Elizabeth Dancy, behind him, his son John and his wife Anne Cresacre. There were eleven grandchildren and a poor relation, Margaret Giggs, also living under his benevolent eye.

Erasmus, practised eulogist, found this family circle perfect. "There is not a man living", he said of his friend, "so affectionate to his children as he" . . . "he loveth his old wife as well as if she was a young maid." As to the daughters "if you should hear them playing skilfully on various instruments of music or watch them poring over every kind of Latin or Greek author like little busy bees . . . you would say they were muses toying sweetly in the loveliest paths of Ionia. . . ." The chronicle of More's son-in-law, William Roper (who lived in the house for as many years as its head), subsequently amplified by More's grandson, Cresacre More, even more authentically pays tribute to the gentle conduct of this Utopia and the piety of Sir Thomas himself. We picture him withdrawn in quiet contemplation in the "New Buildings" (chapel, library and gallery); or in the church (where his chapel survived the air raids of twentieth-century war) singing in the choir "with a surplice on his back", and shocking the Duke of Norfolk on this account ("God's body, my Lord Chancellor, a parish clerk . . .")

Utopias being perfectly disciplined are never free and More's régime was not without its severity. That he suffered none of his servants to play games; strictly segregated the sexes, so that the men and women lived on opposite sides of the house and seldom spoke to each other; and rigidly enforced every religious observance, allowing no absentees from domestic prayer; all this suggests the iron hand. He was charitable to the poor but not to dissenters; and if the story that he bound heretics to the "Jesus Tree" in his Chelsea garden and had them mercilessly flogged is the invention of a protestant martyrology there is evidence enough of a strangely mingled strain in his character of merriment and sternness, kindliness and bigotry.

Even Erasmus became critical on this score: and the slab (that still survives) with its epitaph composed by More to hang over his tomb in the church bears its dramatic witness. There is a gap at one point. The Latin reads "FURIBUS AUTEM ET HOMICIDIS   MOLESTUS". More described himself as the scourge of thieves, murderers—and, in the draft he showed to Erasmus, of (the missing word) "heretics". Erasmus, the humanist, protested against this declaration of intolerance. It is typical of More that he could make the declaration—and also, with a certain humour, defer to his more tolerant friend by leaving the significant blank, for posterity to read into it what they would.

More's last days at Chelsea are most vivid of all. He seems to have had a premonition that in the end his rigid principles would clash with Henry VIII's ruthless absence of principle. One can feel him wince on the day that Roper describes when the King walking in great good humour with More, in the Chelsea garden after dinner flung his arm affectionately round his neck. When Roper commented on this mark of favour, More gave his famous answer. "I find his Grace my very good Lord indeed . . . Howbeit (sonne Roper) I may tell thee I have no cause to be prowde thereof. For yf my head would winne him a Castle in Fraunce (for then there was war between us) yt should not fayle to go."

To resign the Lord Chancellorship, as he did in 1532 was to accept poverty and obscurity. He gave his barge, with its eight watermen, to his successor in office, Lord Audley: his "fool" (he was mediaeval enough to keep one) to the Lord Mayor of London. He spoke of economies in housekeeping with gaiety —they would begin with Lincoln's Inn diet and if that proved too expensive, come down next year to Oxford fare. Yet even in humble retirement, he was forced to commit himself on the issue between Pope and King.

He goes to confession and hear mass in the church one morning in 1535, determined not to take the "Oath of Supremacy and Matrimony" for which purpose he has been summoned to Lambeth. Sadly he shuts the gate in the courtyard so that this time his children shall not see him off from the water's edge. The boat bears him away along Chelsea Reach, determined on the refusal for which he will shortly be beheaded. . . .

He was not, as he had wished, buried in Chelsea. His body, it is to be supposed, remained in the chapel of St. Peter's-within-the-Tower; his head after being impaled on London Bridge was removed to the Roper vault in St. Dunstan's, Canterbury. Yet he is still a presence, not only in national and political but in local history. He enables us to see Tudor Chelsea and in many respects is the prototype of later famous inhabitants. A lover of art, a collector of antiques and curiosities, the patron of Holbein who stayed with him, probably designed the Renaissance capitals in the More chapel (and may be called the first of Chelsea artists). Like Rossetti at No. 16 Cheyne Walk, he had his private menagerie—some rare birds, an ape, a weasel, a ferret. In wit and humour More seems in advance of his time and was capable of witticisms that sometimes have an even Whistlerian ring. Quite worthy of that later Chelsea celebrity is Sir Thomas's answer to the Tower official who hoped he was not too uncomfortable, "You can always turn me out of doors."

The More connection with Chelsea was not quite at an end. After the confiscation of Sir Thomas's estate, poor Lady More, bewildered by what seemed to her the wanton foolishness of her late husband's behaviour and reduced to extreme poverty, was comforted to some extent by the grant of one of his smaller houses in Chelsea. William Roper is mentioned in 1543 as a freeholder of the manor. The King's affection for the district

24

4 Sir Thomas More's chapel in the old church
From an early nineteenth-century watercolour

5 Sir Robert Stanley: detail of the Stanley
monument in the old church

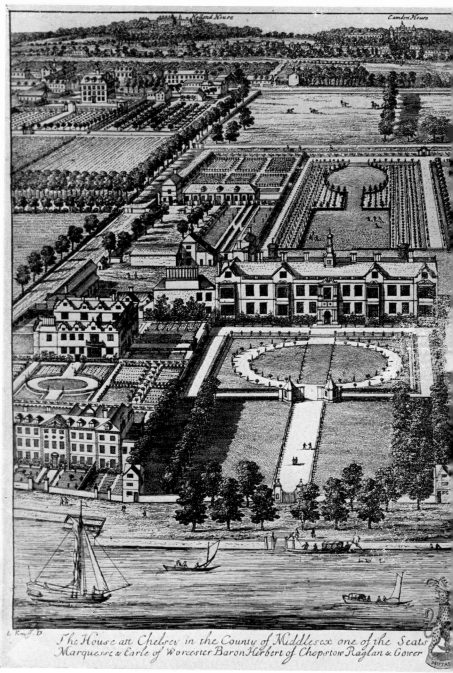

The House att Chelsey in the County of Middlesex one of the Seats
Marquesse & Earle of Worcester Baron Herbert of Chepstow Raglan & Gower

6 Beaufort House, Chelsea, and its garden, about 1707. Originally "The Great
had been made, but substantially in plan and general character was as it was when Sir
On the left is Lindsey

From an engraving by

Kingsinton House

of the Most Noble & Potent Prince Henry Duke of Beaufort and Knight of the Most Noble order of the Garter.

I. Kip Sen.

More House", it had at the date of this print been renovated and some improvements
Thomas More lived there. The little lodges in the forecourt originally had flat roofs.
House (c. 1674)

J. Kip, after L. Knyff, 1699

7 The effigies of Lord Dacre and his wife (1594) in the old church

8 Brass from the Tomb of the Gorges Family (1625), dug up in the old church (1832)

(and perhaps for the memory of More himself) was undiminished. He acquired the manor from Lord Sandys in exchange for Mottisfont Priory in Hampshire and built (1536–7) a new manor-house, standing somewhat to the east of Oakley Street, on Cheyne Walk. Its appearance can scarcely be judged from the engraving in Faulkner's history (taken from an old "roll") but its accommodation when it comprised the adjoining Winchester House is given in the deed of sale by the Parliamentary commissioners in 1653 as "three cellars in the first [ground] floor, three halls, three parlours, three kitchens, two parlours, larders and nine other rooms with a large staircase, in the first story; three drawing rooms, seventeen chambers and four closets [in the second] with garrets over part of them, and summer rooms with a bedroom". Gardens, orchards, stables and coach-house extended the property to five acres. Fragments of garden wall remain, Tudor brickwork is to be found in the lower course of the walls between Nos. 19 and 26 Cheyne Walk: the Survey of London (Chelsea: Part I) detected in their gardens an "air" of the palace pleasure grounds.

Here Henry stayed at intervals and Princess Elizabeth was lodged as a girl, being subjected to the unpleasant advances of Lord Admiral Seymour, who was married to Queen Katharine soon after Henry's death. The unfortunate Lady Jane Grey lived in the Manor House: Anne of Cleves, Henry's fourth wife, died there in 1557: Lord Howard of Effingham, victor of the Spanish Armada, became its tenant in 1585 and was visited there by Queen Elizabeth. The interesting personal histories of these Tudor residents are not, however, so directly relevant to Chelsea as those of later lords of the manor, whose names have become a permanent part of its topography; Cheyne Walk, Cheyne Row . . . they take us back to the year 1657 when Charles Cheyne purchased the manor and settled in Chelsea with his wife, Lady Jane, daughter of the Duke of Newcastle, who brought him a large fortune. She died in 1669 and Dr. Adam Littleton, Rector of Chelsea, gave a funeral sermon paying tribute to her piety, fortitude during the Civil War, and good works. "Of her charity to this place I question but

one shall see in a short time some fair testimonies noted."
Cheyne Walk was so named in her honour. Her husband,
who was made Viscount Newhaven and Lord Cheyne by
Charles II in 1681, and married a second time—the widow of
the Earl of Radnor—continued to take a great interest in Chelsea.
On June 20, 1696, John Evelyn records, "I made my Lord
Cheyney a visit at Chelsea and saw those ingenious waterworks
invented by Mr. Winstanley wherein were some things very
surprising and extraordinary." (Winstanley, engineer and
builder of the Eddystone Lighthouse, was noted for his "mechanic
tricks" so much to seventeenth-century taste.) Lord Cheyne's
concern for the welfare of the parish appears in a letter to the
rector (1698), "The Church doth indeed want a gallery, even
for ye inhabitants you have and I shall be ready to help you to
more, if I could myselfe or gett others to build more houses.
I would be glad to lett land for that purpose, and particularly
put down a tavern and bowling-green, for your designs of better
and more sober purposes . . ." Lord Cheyne's will expressed
the desire that his body should be laid by that of his first wife
"in the vault where there is a place prepared in the chancel
of the parish church of Chelsea under the communion table".
He left his properties to his second wife and his son William:
among the bequests to the latter being "all my lands in
Chelsea commonly called Blacklands" (the present Sloane
Street area).

Sloane Street, Sloane Square, Hans Place . . . another set of
street names commemorates the most famous of the manor's
later lords, Sir Hans Sloane, who bought it in 1712 from
William, Lord Cheyne, second and last Viscount Newhaven.
He was then fifty-two, a famous physician and naturalist, for
many years Secretary of the Royal Society of which he became
President, full of its spirit of scientific enquiry. In many
respects he was a notable pioneer: a first advocate of a national
health service for the poor and one of the early propagandists
of vaccination. He was noted for his study of medicinal and
exotic plants: a visit to Jamaica as physician to the Governor
having produced a catalogue of Jamaican plants (1696) and a

profusely illustrated account of his travels (1707). He had married the rich widow of a Jamaica planter, but acquired considerable wealth by his own professional efforts, devoting large sums to a collection of books, manuscripts, antiquities, curiosities, gems, minerals and botanical specimens which grew to surprising dimensions.

This temperate, wealthy, learned, able and genial man became in the long latter part of his life (he lived to be ninety-three) the same sort of tutelary spirit in Chelsea that More had been. He came to own a large part of the parish, including Beaufort House that had once been More's (though this he pulled down). He transported his collection from Bloomsbury and among the illustrious visitors who went to Chelsea to see it were the Prince and Princess of Wales. Naturally, he took a great interest in the Botanic Garden, where he remains a distinguished presence in the statue by Rysbrack (erected during his lifetime).

Chelsea Place, in his later years when he was confined to a wheeled chair and had long given up his duties as Royal Physician, was in effect a museum. Long tables in the three front rooms carried cases of precious stones. The gallery, 110 feet long, was lined with geological and insect specimens. There were rooms filled with books and volumes of dried plants: "below stairs some rooms were filled with curious remains of antiquities from Egypt, Greece, Etruria, Rome, Britain and even America".

"Sir Hans Sloane is dead", wrote Horace Walpole in 1753, "and has made me one of the trustees to his museum, which is to be offered for 20,000l. to the King, the Parliament, the Royal Academies of Petersburgh, Berlin, Paris and Madrid. He valued it at four score thousand: and so would anybody who loves hippopotamuses, sharks with one ear and spiders big as geese!" "You may think", he added, "that those who think money the most valuable of all curiosities will not be purchasers." Fortunately for the nation, the official view was more enlightened. The collection was bought by the Government (from the proceeds of a lottery) though the Chelsea house was not, as Sir Hans had wished, made its permanent home. Combined with the

Harleian and Cottonian libraries it became the splendid nucleus of the British Museum.

In the manorial pattern of names, that of Cadogan comes next, Sir Hans Sloane having divided his Chelsea estate between his married daughters, Mrs. Stanley and Elizabeth, Lady Cadogan, with a reversion to the Cadogan family. The building programme of the late eighteenth and nineteenth centuries divided the honours of nomenclature. The doctor's Christian name gave "Hans Town"—the ancient "Blacklands"—developed by Henry Holland, architect of the original Brighton Pavilion. The development began (1777) with Holland's house, "The Pavilion", a project for the Brighton scheme, with Doric portico and in the grounds an arrangement of Gothic ruins for which Cardinal Wolsey's house at Esher provided material. It stood in twenty of the hundred acres Holland leased from the Earl of Cadogan but vanished in the wave of subsequent building. There are late Georgian houses still in Hans Place but Hans Town in late Victorian times was a memory erased by the affluence of Cadogan Square.

The centre of Chelsea individualism and personal memory was the Old Church, the parish church of St. Luke until 1819 when the new St. Luke's was built. It then became a Chapel of Ease and reverted to its original dedication, All Saints. This ancient foundation (mentioned in Papal letters of 1290 and 1299 as the Church of "Thelchurche" and "Chelchuthe") like the rest of Chelsea scarcely begins to exist for us before the sixteenth century. Traces of mediaeval work, few enough, were further reduced by the air raid of April 17, 1941 which destroyed the greater part of the fabric, including that most homely and unpretentious of landmarks, the seventeenth-century brick tower and the Lawrence Chapel, once the freehold of the lords of the manor. Fortunately the More Chapel(4) survived almost intact, together with the famous Renaissance capitals, dated 1528, which it is almost certain (from the evidence of style as well as date) were designed by Holbein when staying with More (and perhaps carried out by Italian or Franco-Italian craftsmen, from among those who came to England in Henry VIII's reign).

The Old Church

At the time of writing, the monuments, clustered together in a small space, are more than ever the main focus of interest. There is the plain Gothic altar tomb (1532) of Sir Thomas More (restored by J. Faulkner, "statuary" of Chelsea in 1833) with its celebrated inscription slab, and the appended epigrammatic lines in Latin verse in which his unconventional humour came out. Praising the devotion of his second wife to the children of his first wife, he scarcely knew which was dearer to him:

> O! Simul, O! Iuncti poteramus vivere nos tres
> Quam bene, si Fatum, Religioq Sinant
> At societ tumulus, societ nos obsecro coelum
> Sic Mors, non potuit quod dare, Vita, dabit.

"Ah! how well could we three have lived together, did fate and religion permit. But the tomb shall unite us, I pray, and Death give us what Life could not."

More referred in his own epitaph to resigning the Lord Chancellorship. "He therefore", he wrote of himself, "irked and weary of worldly business, giving up his promotions, attained at last by the incomparable benefit of his most gentle Prince (if it please God to favour his enterprise) that thing, which in a manner from a child he always wished and desired; that he might have some years of his life free, in which he, little and little withdrawing himself from the business of this life, might continually remember the immortality of the life to come." It was the sentiment he put succintly on the day when he went to his wife's pew in the church, after his retirement, and in parody of the phrase used, during his Chancellorship, by one of his gentlemen at the end of the service, himself announced "Madam, my lord is gone."

Other memorials tell us of various lords of the manor, of the inhabitants of More's house in its later form, and the division of his estates on which further mansions were built; some also meriting separate appraisal as interesting examples of sculpture and ornament in the late sixteenth and seventeenthcentury styles.

The tombchest of Sir Reginald Bray is that of the owner of the manor in the time of Henry VII. Sir Reginald, a statesman of some note, and an architect who perhaps designed the Henry VII chapel at Westminster, left a disputable will which resulted in the manor's passing, by agreement, not to his nephew Edmund, as he first planned, but to his niece Margery and so also to her husband, Sir William Sandys, later Baron Sandys, from whom King Henry VIII purchased the property.

The remains of the once magnificent monument (1555) to the Duchess of Northumberland, with Gothic niche and diapered shafts supporting a canopy, with a representation of fan tracery in the soffit, are a reminder of the later Tudor history of the manor. Edward VI granted it in 1553 to John Dudley, Duke of Northumberland, who was executed in the same year for his plot to put Lady Jane Grey and his son, Guildford, on the throne. The Duchess was allowed to stay on at the manorhouse until her death, two or three years later. A remaining brass shows the Duchess with her five daughters, of whom Mary became the mother of Sir Philip Sidney and Catherine, who married the Earl of Huntingdon, died and was buried in the church in 1620. The Richard Jervoise monument (1563), a freestanding arch with heavy strapwork ornament and fluting

34

is, architecturally, an early example of the classic revival and, in human terms, brings us to another phase of the Chelsea family story. The elder Richard Jervoise, apparently a "self-made" man of wealth, lived in the old manor-house after Henry VIII bought it from Lord Sandys. He married Winifred, daughter of a London mercer, John Barnard, whose son, James Barnard, married Ursula, Lord Sandys' daughter. The monument seems to have been erected by Winifred Jervoise on the death of her son, Richard. There are no Barnard monuments; but Ursula re-appears with her second husband, Thomas Hungerford, in the tablet of alabaster and marble (1581) where Hungerford and his two sons face his wife and daughter in conventional kneeling posture.

A similar memorial is that of Thomas Lawrence (1598). The Lawrences, who gave their name to the Lawrence Chapel in the church and also to Lawrence Street, were a family whose obscure but not uninteresting history has been patiently examined by Mr. Randall Davies in his *Chelsea Old Church*. They acquired the old manor-house between 1557 and 1587 and were great people in Chelsea for some 150 years or until the death (1725) of Margaret, daughter of Sir Thomas Lawrence (appointed Secretary to Maryland, 1691, buried at Chelsea, 1714). The wall tablet with its kneeling figures commemorates Thomas Lawrence, goldsmith. The monument (dated 1631—it should be 1632) to his eldest daughter, Sarah, who married Richard Colvile of Newton in the Isle of Ely, is the most striking in the church. Shroud-clad, the alabaster half-length figure rises from a coffin of black marble. The combination of the physical and the ecstatic echoes in another medium the metaphysical poetry of the age and resembles that in certain other early seventeenth-century English funerary sculptures (like Nicholas Stone's John Donne in St. Paul's).

The monument to Gregory, Lord Dacre (1594) and his wife, Anne (1595)(7) draws attention to the fate of More's house. After his execution, it passed to William Pawlet, subsequently Marquis of Winchester, who died there in 1572. His son, John, married (a second time) Winifred, daughter of Sir John Burgess and widow of Sir Robert Sackville. Winifred's daughter, Anne Sackville, married Gregory, Lord Dacre, and obtained the Chelsea estates, to the annoyance of the third Marquis of Winchester, by a sharp piece of bargaining. (She contrived, according to a document found by Mr. Randall Davies among the State Papers, to buy the house and land for a fraction of their value.) The recumbent figures of their tomb, he in armour, she in ruff, mantle and bonnet, lie in a recess beneath a structure that is cumbrous and topheavy, with its "pyramids of freckied marble", heraldic emblems and its crowning allegory of Time, Death and Judgment, but impressive in its Elizabethan ornateness.

The More estates later belonged to Sir Arthur Gorges. Lady Dacre left her Chelsea property to Lord Burleigh: from him it went to his son, Sir Robert Cecil, who rebuilt the house in 1597 but sold it, after two years, to Henry, Earl of Lincoln. Gorges, third son of Sir William Gorges, Vice-Admiral of the Fleet, and one of the Elizabethan seamen who volunteered for service against the Armada, married Lincoln's daughter and thus acquired the whole estate, including the More chapel and the satellite mansion perhaps already built by Lincoln, but known as Gorges House. In the church a brass (1625)(8) shows him kneeling in prayer with his wife and family. Gorges House later became Milman House, after Sir William Milman, (commemorated by a tablet, 1713) who gave his name to Milman Street. Sir Arthur Gorge's daughter, Elizabeth, married Sir Robert Stanley, son of the sixth Earl of Derby. They occupied a house called Brickhills on the site of Stanley Grove, later residence of the Principal of St. Mark's College.

Sir Robert Stanley provides the most grandiose of the church's monuments, splendid in its way, though the alabaster figures of Justice and Fortitude may have been an afterthought and a little confuse the spacious composition. The central urn surmounted by the eagle of the Stanley crest is fine, so are the medallion busts of Sir Robert(5), and (on either side) his infant children, Ferdinando and Henrietta. The eagle motif comes into their epitaph:

The Eagle Death greedie of some good prey
With nimble Eyes found where these Infants laye
He truste them in his Tallents and conveyde
There Soules to Heaven & here theire ashes layde.

Matching in impressiveness the Dacre, Colvile and Stanley monuments is that (1672) of Charles Cheyne, Viscount Newhaven, and his first wife, Lady Jane, who owned the manor after the Civil War, the lady's benefactions permitting the completion of the new church fabric and tower some years after her death in 1669. The monument was made in Rome, letters discovered by Mr. Randall Davies in the Bridgewater MS. indicating that the architect was the great Bernini's son, Paolo and the sculptor of the reclining figure of the lady, Antonio Raggi, who worked from drawings sent him. The collaboration was not aesthetically perfect. The architectural frame tends to obscure the figure: the recess is too equally divided by sarcophagus and sculpture, but the result has suitable dignity.

The manorial record ends with the surviving monument in the churchyard (1753) to Sir Hans Sloane, erected by his two daughters, Eliza Cadogan and Sarah Stanley, and designed by Joseph Wilton (1722–1803), who was also responsible for the tablet in the church (1781) to Lucy Smith and Anne Wilton, apparently his daughters. We advance then from the period of close-knit relationships and family pomp to the simpler memorials of artist and writer, noting in particular the calligraphic tablet dedicated to William Frend De Morgan (1917):

ARTIST—POTTER—INVENTOR—NOVELIST
BORN 16TH NOVEMBER 1839   DIED 15TH JANUARY 1917

who did much of his best work in Cheyne Row, the Vale and Church Street, Chelsea—where he died.

Recreating in Ceramic work upon his own vigorous designs the colour of the Persian & the lustre of the great Umbrian craftsmen Enriching literature by his faithful & sympathetic presentment of homely and very human character And beloved by all *w*ho kne*w* his breadth of intellectual interest, his catholic sympathy, genial humour & lambent *w*it.

And the tablet (1916)

IN MEMORY OF
HENRY JAMES O : M
NOVELIST
BORN IN NEW YORK 1843: DIED IN
CHELSEA 1916: LOVER AND INTER⁄
PRETER OF THE FINE AMENITIES
OF BRAVE DECISIONS & GENEROUS
LOYALTIES: A RESIDENT OF THIS
PARISH WHO RENOUNCED A
CHERISHED CITIZENSHIP TO GIVE
HIS ALLEGIANCE TO ENGLAND IN
THE 1ST YEAR OF THE GREAT WAR

In his Chelsea novel, *The Hillyars and the Burtons*, Henry Kingsley, who spent his childhood in the rectory, fittingly describes the church as a combination of historic personalities. "'Four hundred years of memory', says Joe Burton, 'are crowded into that old church, and the great flood of change beats round the walls, and shakes the door in vain but never enters. The dead stand thick together there, as if to make a brave resistance to the moving world outside, which jars upon their slumber. It is a church of the dead.'"

II

TOWN OF PALACES

WRITERS on Chelsea have had a fondness for the title "Village of Palaces", though "Town of Palaces" was the phrase originally coined by Defoe in his *Tour through England and Wales* (1724–6) in which he reflected on the narrowing space between Chelsea and London. "A town of palaces, and which by its new extended buildings seems to promise itself to be made one time or other a part of London, I mean London in its new extended capacity, which if it should happen, what a monster must London be, extending (to take it in a line) from the farther end of Chelsea, west, to Deptford Bridge east, which I venture to say, is at least eleven miles."

In his time its popularity among the great and wealthy was assured and increasing. It had received Stuart no less than Tudor approval. Charles II favoured it as Henry VIII had done. He swam gaily in the Thames "over against Chelsea", careless of the Irish adventurer, Colonel Blood, who lurked with a gun in the reeds on the Battersea side, waiting to take a shot at him. According to tradition he visited Nell Gwynn at Sandford Manor just over the Fulham border. A rough track across the fields was converted into his private road—it officially became the King's Road in 1713. The court followed him; so fashionable was Chelsea that it was known as "Hyde Park on Thames": and this fashionable phase lasted well into the eighteenth century. The series of great houses gave Chelsea a distinguished profile. Greatest of them was that which had been More's, Beaufort House, where Beaufort Street now is. Its "Kitchen yard or garden" on the west extended to the backyard and buildings of Gorges House (the clustered Elizabethan gables of which can be seen in Kip's engraving). Adjoining, on the west, the forecourt of Beaufort House, was Lindsey House, the one seventeenth-century mansion that has survived until the present day(10).

39

Originally More's principal farmhouse, rebuilt, according to Chelsea's earliest historian, Bowack (1705), by Sir Theodore Mayerne, physician to Charles I, "after the modern manner", probably rebuilt again by the third Earl of Lindsey in 1674, it still looks, in spite of subsequent changes, very like the plain three-storied house depicted with such admirable precision in the Kip engraving of 1699(6). Danvers House flanked Beaufort House on the east. Possibly the "New Buildings" with chapel and library to which More had retired for meditation, reconstructed in 1623 by Sir John Danvers, it is part of the insubstantial pageant of vanished architecture on which, with the help of Aubrey's description, it is pleasant to linger. A quaint old house in his time "not according to the staid perfection of Roman architecture now in vogue": but certainly—a house of culture. In the days before the Civil War, the King's Musick performed for Sir John in the "stately Roome" above the Hall, with Dr. Gibbons at the "excellent organ of stoppes of cedar". Danvers laid out the "great gravelled walks of the Garden" in Italian style. One imagines him there, pointing out the merits of Nicholas Stone's sculptures of Cain and Abel, or brushing his beaver hat on the borders of hyssop and thyme to "perfume it with their natural essence".

Among other architectural phantoms of Chelsea are: the Lawrence House to the north of Lordship Yard, possibly on the site of the old manor house; known in its later days as Monmouth House, having been leased by the widow of Sir Thomas Lawrence (d. 1712) to Ann, Duchess of Monmouth: Shrewsbury House (west of Oakley Street) which took its name from George, Earl of Shrewsbury (henchman of Henry VIII), dated back to Henry's reign and was long confused with More's house: Winchester House, adjoining Henry VIII's manor-house, built about the middle of the seventeenth century by James, Duke of Hamilton, the palace of the Bishops of Winchester until the end of the eighteenth century, two-storied, of plain red brick, but with an entrance hall forty feet long and a grand staircase leading to three drawing-rooms extending the whole length of the south front: Gough House, in Tite Street, built

9 "Whistler's House", No. 96 Cheyne Walk, formerly the east wing
of Lindsey House

10 Nos. 96 to 106 Cheyne Walk, with, in the centre, Lindsey House (built about 1674)

(*c.* 1707) by the third Earl of Carberry (who made a fortune in the slave trade) but taking its name from its subsequent owner, Sir Richard Gough, a wealthy merchant, and now merged into the Victoria Hospital for Children: adjoining Gough House with beautiful gardens to the river, Walpole House, built about 1690, improved for Sir Robert Walpole by Sir John Vanbrugh, whose additions were almost certainly the part of the house incorporated in Sir John Soane's Infirmary (1810) for the Royal Hospital, though of the Infirmary, bombed out during the Second World War, fragments only remain.

Seen from the Thames, gay and lively then with any number of small craft (as no doubt Defoe saw it) the line of stately brick mansions with their lawns and flowered walks reaching riverwards, must have been unique in effect. Eastward, and com-pleting its harmony, was what Defoe well called, "the noblest building and the best foundation of its kind in the world", the Royal Hospital. And, as a palatial outpost on the London side of the Hospital, there was the house built (about 1690) by Charles II's favourite, Richard Jones, Earl of Ranelagh, with gardens and land totalling twenty-three acres, the "little palace, I had almost called it a paradise", said Defoe, "of the late Earl of Ranelagh" (*d.* 1712).

Away from the river, the mansions were fewer and smaller. They included the (existing) Argyll House (No. 211 King's Road), built 1723 by the Venetian architect Giacomo Leoni for John Perrin (or Pierene), though taking its name from John, fourth Duke of Argyll who lived there in his last years, 1769–70. Grand, though small, is what Leoni called "this little House of my Invention", with its delightful wrought-iron gate, its stone doorway comprising Tuscan three-quarter columns, Doric entablature, urns and balustrade, and within a beautifully spacious staircase. The architect congratulated himself on the, to him, novel harmony he obtained between gray brick and white stone.

Also in the King's Road is Stanley House, the property being in the possession of the Stanleys until the death of the last of the line, William, in 1691. The new house, built some years after and perhaps not completed until the beginning of the eighteenth century, is a good, sensible building, with an interior doorway, supported by Ionic columns and having a broken pediment, that achieves magnificence.

No trace remains of the famous seventeenth-century houses in the region of the Fulham Road, at the then hamlet known as "Little Chelsea": of Shaftesbury House, originally built by Sir James Smith in 1635, altered about 1700, by Anthony Ashley Cooper, third Earl of Shaftesbury and author of *The Characteristics of Men, Manners, Opinions and Times*. It was occupied by him until, suffering from asthma, he was driven by the "great smoake" of Chelsea northwards to Hampstead. Or of the house with its fine laboratory where Robert Boyle the physicist lived and was visited by Evelyn in 1661; where "glasses, potts, chymical and mathematical instruments, books and bundles of papers did so fill and crowd his bed-chamber, that there was but just room for a few chairs".

A corollary of the "palace" was a form of palace life and it is needful to imagine the gay and courtly humanity, especially after the Restoration, of which the catalogue of mansions is a projection. The exquisite rooms were full of courtiers and court ladies, posing, gossiping, intriguing. There was a constant round of receptions, festivals and entertainments; like the "very sumptuous treat" given by the Duke of Monmouth in the summer of 1673 for "Madame Carwell" (Louise de Quérouaille), Charles II's mistress, then lately made Duchess of Portsmouth, the treat being accompanied by fireworks and illuminations. The flow of life through the vanished (smaller) houses of Paradise Row (now Royal Hospital Road) has been admirably described in his *Paradise Row* by the late Mr. Reginald Blunt; whose pen sketched its characters with so much appreciation, sadly for whom the camera recorded in 1906 the last of the beautiful doorways, at Nos. 5, 6 and 7, remaining from the end of the seventeenth century and due for demolition.

The person and the household of Mazarin's niece (Hortense Mancini) have all that vividness which belongs to this village of long memories: the self-styled Duchesse de Mazarin was certainly the most spectacular inhabitant of Paradise Row. She had a stormy past, had fled to Italy in man's clothes to escape from her obnoxious husband, Duc de la Meilleraye. An intimate of Charles II in the days of his exile she remained so after her arrival in England in 1675 (aged twenty-eight), receiving a "Secret Service" allowance of £4,000 a year, but spending so recklessly on gambling and display, that she was always in arrear with the poor rate, and it was a well understood thing that guests at dinner might leave money under their plates. A foil to the personality of this wild, black-haired, dark-blue-eyed beauty was that of the Seigneur de Saint-Evremond, another refugee in Chelsea, barred from France for political sarcasms on the Peace of the Pyrenees but welcomed by Charles and esteemed as much in London as in literary Paris for his satirical and elegant prose, though he never learnt to speak the language of his adopted country and, unlike Voltaire, did not attempt to read Shakespeare. Thirty-seven years older than the Duchesse (though he long outlived her, reaching the age of ninety-three) he lodged in her house, not quite a lover—or a father—but a philosopher deeply attached to the object of his study, regarding with indulgent interest her losses at basset, her pets—the parrot "Pretty", the dog "Chop" and the cat "Monsieur Poussy"—the course of her relations with the King, and with that unfortunate Swedish baron whom her nephew killed in a duel. Their joint salon has been described not only by Faulkner but by Sainte-Beuve also. In the words of our Chelsea historian it was "daily frequented by the principal nobility and persons of wit and genius". There, says Faulkner, "in the style of free conversation, were discussed subjects of the deepest specu-lation, such as philosophy, and religion, history, poetry, criticism, on dramatic and other compositions, and the niceties of the French language". Variety was provided by the card-table where "an obscure man named Morin" acted as banker, and by elaborate musical and dramatic performances which seem to have encouraged the introduction of Italian Opera into England.

Another dweller in Paradise Row was Betty Becke, whose attraction for Lord Sandwich was considered so regrettable by Samuel Pepys, that in 1663 he wrote the nobleman a tremendous letter of reproof. Sandwich, according to Pepys, in his fit of morality, did "grossly play the fool". "His daughters do perceive all and do hate the place and the young woman", though Pepys, on meeting her in the following year, wondered "the less at my Lord's favour to her", finding that while "she hath not one good feature in her face", yet she was "a fine lady, of a fine taille" and "I dare warrant she hath brains enough to entangle him". Did Nell Gwynn live in Paradise Row? is a question that Chelsea historians have asked—with all that tenderness that the most puritanical of Britons display towards "frailty" at a distance of a century or two but her link with the region is vague. It is not certain that she lived at Sandford Manor; nor is there any evidence that she urged on Charles the foundation of a hospital for the poor soldiers; but her son by him, made first Duke of St. Albans, lived in the Row and her reputed presence in Stuart Chelsea invests local tradition with a cheerful warmth, such as a star of the music-hall might leave behind. By way of contrast, Paradise Row had its militant bluestocking in a younger contemporary and neighbour of the Duchesse de Mazarin, Mary Astell (buried in the old church), daughter of a Newcastle merchant and author of a *Serious Proposal to the Ladies*, advocating a lay religious retreat for Church of England women.

The hospitality and entertainments of the town of palaces were lavish; lights, music and the river made its hospitable occasions splendid. A memorable banquet was that given for George I one August evening in 1715 by Lady Catherine Jones, unmarried daughter of Lord Ranelagh, who inherited Ranelagh House; when a fanciful flotilla brought the Royal party in decorative barges, accompanied by hundreds of small boats sparkling with coloured lights in the blue dusk. Handel himself conducted his water music, played by an orchestra of fifty, from one of the City barges; and music and banqueting went on in the house until two in the morning.

Equally splendid were the entertainments at Walpole House, where Sir Robert Walpole spent a good deal of time between about 1722 and 1746, appearing there as cultivated and charming host rather than cynical statesman. Pope described this "happier hour" when he had

> Seen him uncumbered by the venal tribe,
> Smile without art, and win without a bribe.

Here he received Queen Caroline and members of the Royal Family in August, 1729. A temporary kitchen was built in the stable-yards with twenty fireplaces to prepare the dinner, set out in the greenhouse or orangery designed by Vanbrugh. After it, the royal visitors took tea in the octagon summer-house overlooking the Thames, while musicians stationed in barges played for them; no doubt admired the gardens and the grotto devised by Lady Walpole in emulation of Pope's grotto at Twickenham, and looked at the paintings in the house (later to form part of the Imperial Gallery at St. Petersburg); returning finally to the greenhouse for the Ball and the supper that accompanied it.

> Go with old Thames, view Chelsea's glorious pile,
> And ask the shattered hero whence his smile.
> Rogers, *The Pleasures of Memory*

If a palace be defined as a spacious building for entertainment (not necessarily of an ostentatious kind), the incomparably greatest palace of Chelsea was, and is, the Royal Hospital designed by Sir Christopher Wren. In examining its origin we must revert for a moment to Nell Gwynn, whose name is a quite modern edition to the List of Benefactors in the Great Hall. A portrait "after Lely" hung there until recently, though the original (National Portrait Gallery) is now adjudged to be neither of her nor by Lely. Legend has it that Charles II, when the site was discussed, recalled he had promised the land to her; that she, generously, offered it back again. Documentary evidence is against it and John Evelyn, certainly one of

47

the scheme's main promoters, makes no mention of any such interchange: but whether or not it took place, the Hospital was historically inevitable.

In the Middle Ages, the old and infirm, including super-annuated and disabled soldiers, were accommodated in the hostels or hospitals largely supported by the monasteries. The dissolution of the monasteries threw the onus of support on private charity which was bound to be inadequate. Since Tudor times there had been many complaints of the neglect of "maymed souldieres". The beginning of a regular army in Charles II's reign demanded state planning; a hospital for soldiers to which that for sailors at Greenwich was a later complement.

At Chelsea there was a suitable site, the ground on which stood the remnants of an unlucky enterprise, the Theological College, founded in 1618 with the sanction of James I. It was intended to house twenty learned doctors warring on the "pedantry, sophistries and novelties of the jesuits and others", likewise "the treachery of pelagians and arminians". Archbishop Laud aptly filed correspondence concerning it under the heading "Contro-versy College". As a building, it was curiously planned and never completed; as an idea, it did not come off. The Puritans suspected it; the Commonwealth turned it into a military prison: "a cage for unclean birds" as the Rev. J. Darley complained. Scottish prisoners of the Civil War were first housed there; then prisoners taken in the wars with Holland. It was Evelyn's job to supervise the place: hence the entry in his diary, January 8, 1665: "I visited our prisoners at Chelsey College and to examine how the marshal and sutlers behaved. These were prisoners taken in the war; they only complained their bread was too fine." Conditions later worsened. The prisoners went hungry; plague broke out among them; as the Dutch ambassador, Van Gogh, feared, a number found a way out by volunteering to fight under the English. In 1667, no longer used as a prison, what was left of the College was turned over to the Royal Society as a gift from the King.

For many years it stayed derelict while the Royal Society wondered what to do with it: being much relieved in 1682 when the King bought it back for £1,300. What Nell Gwynn would have done with the "roofless ruin" is speculative—though a heavy charge on the Secret Service funds might have been foreseen; but meanwhile Evelyn and Sir Stephen Fox, first Army Paymaster-General, had concerted the hospital plan.

It had a recent precedent; the foundation stone of the Hospital for the army in Ireland, at Kilmainham, near Dublin, was already (1680) laid. Fox "who had", says Evelyn, "gotten so vast an estate by the soldiers" (by paying them out of his own pocket and charging interest of a shilling in the pound), was anxious to assume the role of benefactor. He and Evelyn drew up a list of officials and salaries (the official continuance of Fox's system of deductions largely financed the Hospital until Victorian times). Evelyn "would needs have a library and mentioned several books, since some soldiers might possibly be studious when they were at leisure to recollect" (1682). With Sir Christopher Wren as architect, from that date the scheme went forward with great speed, though the buildings were not completed until 1691, and not until 1693 did Wren who, as Surveyor-General (and President of the Royal Society), had given his services gratis, receive from William III a grant for his "Paines" of £1,000. By that time 476 non-commissioned officers and men (the number of in-pensioners has remained fairly constant) were installed under a modified form of military organisation. Wren was one of the Board of Commissioners, which has always remained a civil authority. There have been no major changes in the building as a whole, which is generally acknowledged to be one of Wren's most masterly achievements, though the approach and general aspect from a distance were probably rather more impressive in the seventeenth century than they are today. The northern approach is complicated by the interposition of two roads, Royal Hospital Road and St. Leonard's Terrace between the north façade and Royal Avenue, laid out by Wren, though its date and axial direction discredit the theory that it was intended as a stately boulevard leading to Kensington Palace. The original forecourt, now Burton's

The Royal Hospital

Court, thus became a separate piece of ground, though it still belongs to the Hospital and is used for recreation.

The south aspect from the river, also, was evidently much more impressive when the formal gardens, laid out between 1687 and 1692, extended to the river; and from the river-steps, along the broad avenue, bordered by "Kanalls with fish and fowles" there was an unimpeded vista to the great quadrangle and the south front of Chapel and Hall(11).

That a certain reticence accompanies the majesty of design has often been noted and is not an adverse criticism. Thomas Carlyle, in his unusual venture into aesthetic judgment, well remarked: "I had passed it almost daily for many years without thinking much about it, and one day I began to reflect that it had always been a pleasure to me to see it, and I looked at it more attentively and saw that it was quiet and dignified and the work of a gentleman." With New England's suspicion of splendour, and possibly some national prejudice against a building that contained flags taken at Bladensburg and Fort Niagara, Nathaniel Hawthorne (in *Our Old Home*) conceded that "the effect is by no means that of grandeur, which is somewhat disagreeably an attribute of Greenwich Hospital, but a quiet and venerable neatness". It was entirely Wren's own conception, unlike Greenwich where he had to reconcile his work with existing buildings and the design of other architects. It took little from the slightly earlier and similar foundation, the Hôtel des Invalides in Paris (though Charles II may have wished to rival it). In comparison with Mansart's dome, Wren's central cupola seems almost too modest. If one looks for some part of its inspira, tion outside England, it may more obviously be traced to the sober brick buildings of the Dutch: though Wren never went to Holland, Evelyn did, bringing back architectural books and prints, and it is not at all unlikely that in their discussions these came under review.

Yet the gentlemanliness on which Carlyle commented may otherwise be defined as a beautiful appropriateness or "fitness to purpose". The simplicity of the plan derives from the monastic infirmary with its connecting hall and chapel and adjoining quadrangular alms-houses (it was to indicate the size of the proposed building that Evelyn referred to the quadrangle of Christ Church, Oxford). The Hall (115 feet by 38 feet) and Chapel (113 feet by 38½ feet) are separated only by the domed vestibule; the Hall, formerly used as recreation and reading-room being now re-equipped as a refectory (as it is depicted by Pugin and Rowlandson). The two wings at either end four storeys high, divided into corridors lined with wooden cubicles and terminating in the houses of Governor and Lieutenant-Governor, nicely solved the problem of accommodation, and made, with the northern block and its loggia, a dignified enclosure, the main or "Figure" court where the bronze statue of Charles II in Roman dress, by Grinling Gibbons, stands. The four pavilions, added 1688-9, absorbed the residential overflow, without dis-turbing the architectural composition, creating subsidiary courts on either side with pleasant effect.

Wren's attention to "fitness" may be seen in such a detail as the pitch of the staircases, made easy for old limbs (treads, 15 inches wide, risers, 5 inches high): while the oaken cubicles have their privacy ensured by a panel that can be opened or obscured at will. It is all very homely—but that is as it was intended to be.

There is nothing of the museum or "gallery" about the Hospital, though the beauty of functional detail is amply present—in the wrought-iron gates at the main north entrance, the lamp standards in the shape of Ionic columns (east and west courts), the altar rails with their carved foliage in the Chapel, the silver-gilt altar-plate (by Ralph Leete, 1687-8), the appointments of the Council Chamber (with additions by Robert Adam when Clerk of Works). Paintings, however, are few. The huge, dusky picture, at one end of the Hall, of Charles II on horseback, with the Hospital in the background, begun by Verrio and finished by an English follower of Salvator Rosa, Henry Cooke, has never aroused enthusiasms. Nor until recent times has the painting of the Resurrection, in the half-dome of the apse in the Chapel, by the able Venetian artists Sebastiano and Marco Ricci. Hawthorne, with a typical aversion from the baroque, could not "trouble himself to make out the subject". What Dr. Pevsner has called "a splendid piece of Venetian *brio*" is a rediscovery of the twentieth century. There is no collection of military pictures to match the naval pictures of Greenwich—though sea warfare undeniably has the advantage of the land in art, and the absence of such a collection can cause only mild regret. The standards hanging in Chapel and Hall (described and illustrated in the MS. book compiled in 1841 by Captain J. Ford, Captain of Invalids; of which one copy belongs to the Hospital and another is in the Chelsea Public Library) were long a stirring enough reminder of historic campaigns.

The history of the Hospital since Wren's time has been fairly uneventful, architectural changes minor. Robert Adam, 1783-6, replaced the mullioned windows of the wings, with their tran-soms and small panes, by sash windows. Walpole's house, the entrance to which was through the Hospital stable-yard, was assimilated and the Infirmary designed by Sir John Soane in 1810: the obelisk by Cockerell, commemorating the desperate Battle of Chillianwallah was added in 1849. Scars have been left by war; the north-east pavilion, bombed by a Zeppelin in 1918 and rebuilt, was again destroyed by a rocket in 1945: the east wing was damaged in 1940, the Infirmary, in which there were many casualties, bombed out in 1941. Otherwise the buildings have mellowed with age, the green slates of the roofs, the warm red brick of the walls and the Portland stone and wood of the porticoes combining in rich harmony.

Among famous names, apart from those of its architect and sponsors, associated with the Hospital, is that of Dr. Charles Burney, its organist for many years. He, as his daughter, Fanny, records, in 1791 "resided entirely at Chelsea College ['the College' has remained its traditional description]; and he found his sojourn so perfectly to his taste, that though obliged some years afterwards, to remove from the ground-floor to nearly the highest range of rooms in that lofty edifice, he never wished to change the place of his abode". Here "completely to his satis-faction . . . he placed his learned, classical, scientific and miscellaneous library"; when he died, in 1814, he was interred in the Hospital burial ground.

Few unusual happenings, save those of wartime, have disturbed the even tenor of the Hospital's life, though the Hall, in 1808, saw the trial of General Whitelock for bad generalship and in 1852 the lying-in-state of the Duke of Wellington. The veterans, in their uniform that takes us back to the time of Marlborough's campaigns, have lived out their days in peace: and with a dignity that Herkomer's once celebrated, sentimental painting, *The Last Muster*, depicting them assembled in chapel, somewhat mis-represents.

*   *   *

The replacement of one architectural profile by another, the decline and disappearance of most of the palaces, the con-temporaneous, and subsequent, rise of smaller, domestic buildings; is a phase of Chelsea's story that requires to be traced in detail.

The great houses passed through a succession of noble hands and then, one by one, were pulled down, Danvers House, scene of brilliant entertainments in the reign of Charles II, which Pepys considered "the prettiest contrived house I ever saw in my life", was the first to go. Occupied 1660–85 by John, Lord

Robarts, who became Earl of Radnor and, according to Anthony Hamilton, "an old dog, snarling and peevish" with the beautiful young (second) wife, Laetitia, who later married Lord Cheyne, it passed after his death to the Marquis of Wharton and his wife (who wrote a poetical paraphrase of the Lamentations of Jeremiah). Their marriage was childless and unhappy. The house was demolished in 1720, the lands that went with it were sold to Benjamin Stallwood, builder, who began to build Danvers Street as early as 1696. Part of the Danvers estate, in the early eighteenth century, saw the incursion of industry; in 1721 a silk manufactory, in 1723 the tapestry works of Christopher Le Blon.

The More house, rebuilt 1597, by Sir Robert Cecil was successively occupied by the Earl of Lincoln, Sir Arthur Gorges and his wife, Lionel Cranfield, Earl of Middlesex, who lost favour with Charles I and was forced to give up the house to the first Duke of Buckingham. The Duchess lived there after his assassination; the Parliamentary Commissioners, Sir Bulstrode Whitelocke and John Lisle followed, during the Commonwealth period; the second Duke of Buckingham recovered the property after the Restoration, when it was known as Buckingham House, though in 1664 he had to part with it to his creditors. It was then sold to the Earl of Bristol, whose widow sold it in 1682 to the Marquis of Worcester, later Duke of Beaufort, after John Evelyn had unsuccessfully tried to sell it for her. It was, he noted privately, "large but ill-contrived": but in writing to the Earl of Ossory he termed it "magnificent . . . capable of being made (with small expense) perfectly modish . . . The fruits of the garden are exquisite; there is a snow-house—in a word I know of no place more capable of being made the envie of all the noble retreates of the greatest persons neere this court and citty." And a bargain at £3,500. As Beaufort House, it was occasionally occupied by the family until about 1720. Then the Beauforts lost interest; for years it stood empty until in 1737 it was bought by Sir Hans Sloane.

Sloane, who bought Beaufort House for £2,500, seems to have had no intention of living in it, but merely, on principle

11   The River Front

From an engraving after E. Dayes (1797)

12   The Entrance Front

From an engraving after Thomas Malton (1775)

THE ROYAL HOSPITAL

13   The Royal Hospital

From a print published by John Bowles

of extending his estate; and his posthumous praises are tempered by disapproval of his ruthless destruction of the place. Beaufort Row, later Beaufort Street, was laid out on the site in 1766. Only a wall in the Moravian Burial Ground (the stable-yard of Beaufort House) and a wall midway between Beaufort Street and Danvers Street, once dividing the two houses' gardens, have been left to the twentieth century on the site; though Inigo Jones's gateway (1621), perhaps that facing towards King's Road in Kip's engraving, is now at Chiswick as Pope's lines explain:

> Oh gate, how com'st thou here?
>> I was brought from Chelsea last year, [1737]
>> Battered with wind and weather;
>> Inigo Jones put me together,
> Sir Hans Sloane
> Let me alone,
>> Burlington brought me hither.

It is tempting to linger over the personal history of the Gorges (outlined by Mr. Randall Davies in his *Chelsea Old Church*): of Sir Arthur, the typical Elizabethan in his combination of poetry and adventure by sea, the translator of Lucan's *Pharsalia*, the friend of Spenser;* of Timoleon Gorges, his son (whom Spenser might have named), the Fellow of All Souls who met his death in a duel; of the sadly short-lived daughter, Ambrosia, of other descendants—but here it must be enough to say that the house was sold about 1664 and became a school. Josias Priest, "Dancing Master, who kept a Boarding-School of Gentlewomen in Leicester Fields", removed to what was already "the great School-House at Chelsey" in 1680: and the young ladies took part in the first performance of Purcell's opera *Dido and Aeneas*, given there, with words by Nahum Tate and an epilogue by Tom D'Urfey. The house reverted to domestic use when Sir William Milman bought it about 1697 and remained with this family until pulled down to make way for "a new row of buildings

* His collected poems, the "sweet layes of love", perhaps, of which Colin Clout speaks, edited by Professor Helen Sandison, were published early in 1954.

intended to be called Milman's Row" in 1726. The old manor-house, long the home of the Lawrences, was pulled down in the early years of the eighteenth century; between 1704 and 1750 Lawrence Street came into being. The sites of Henry VIII's manor-house, Winchester House and Shrewsbury House gave us Cheyne Walk and Cheyne Row. Shrewsbury House (1543) was not pulled down until 1813. A school at the beginning of the eighteenth century, and later a wall-paper manufactory it is still "Shrewsbury House" (modern flats). Part of its garden wall still remains at the back of Cheyne Row: "Nothing I know of", said Carlyle in 1867, "is more lasting than a well-made brick—we have them here, at the head of this garden (wall once of a manor park) which are in their third or fourth century (Henry VIII's time I am told), and still perfect in every particular." Winchester House disappeared in the early nine-teenth century (1828) and its site is occupied by modern houses and by Oakley Street. The manor-house survived until the death in 1753 of Sir Hans Sloane who took up permanent residence in 1742, though he had bought the house and land in 1712 and as early as 1717 had leased part of the eastern end of what is now Cheyne Walk for building. After Sloane's death, a row of mid-eighteenth century houses (Nos. 19–26, Cheyne Walk) replaced the manor. Cheyne Row dates back to 1708 when William, Lord Cheyne, sold the land for building. Cheyne Walk was a later name, eventually given to the whole length of the old main thoroughfare of Chelsea (which had comprised "Lombard Street" and "Duke Street").

Some curious changes were involved in the decline from courtly life. Where the Duchesse de Mazarin had lived in Paradise Row, Miss Elizabeth Fry established in 1825 her reformatory for girls (which remained there until 1890). Ormond House, at the east end of Paradise Row, home of the Duchess of Ormond, became a Naval Academy in 1779. Shaftesbury House at Little Chelsea became a workhouse, though it remained in its original condition until pulled down in 1856. In 1860 T. C. Croker (*Walk from London to Fulham*) wrote, with a keen sense of incongruity, of "the trim gardens of Queen Anne's time . . . the antique summer

houses ... the little leaden infant Hercules which spouted water
to cool the air from a serpent's throat ... all this too in the garden
of a London Parish Workhouse! Not less surprising was the
interior. The grotesque workshop of the pauper artisans, said
to have been Lord Shaftesbury's doing, and over which was his
famous library, was then an apartment appropriated to a girl's
school ... nor should the apartment then occupied by the
intelligent master of the workhouse be overlooked. The panelling
of the room, its chimney-piece and the painting and framework
above it placed so completely as in a chamber of the time of
William III. ..."

Nor would one have expected a Chelsea mansion to become
the headquarters of a Czech religious brotherhood, yet this was
the fate of Lindsey House between 1751 and 1770, when
occupied by Count Zinzendorf, the "Bishop" of the Moravians
(who were not without their influence on the English Methodists).
It is probable that this early seventeenth-century house was
rebuilt or refronted by the Earl of Lindsey in 1674 and came,
in this condition, to the Count who planned it as the centre of a
utopian colony to be called "Sharon". "The Count's house at
Chelsey is a palace for a prince", wrote John Wesley in 1769,
adding, somewhat cryptically, "Truly are they wise in their
generation." All that remains of "Sharon" is the austere little
area of the Moravian Burial Ground at the end of Milman's
Street: nor did the Count make any drastic alterations to the
house. These came later when it was divided (1775) into separate
dwellings (now Nos. 96–100, Cheyne Walk). The cupolas,
the balustrade to the roof, the pediment with its coats of arms,
the iron gates and piers then disappeared. Front doors were
inserted: yet here, in an excellent state of preservation (1954) the
framework of a seventeenth-century mansion remains visible.
The conclusion of the tale of demolition is that "Old Chelsea",
so rich in earlier memories, is, as far as it still exists, an architectural product of the eighteenth century, though it has seemed
to retain a certain Dutch flavour which belonged to the reign of
William and Mary and to the Hospital of Wren. In the middle
of the seventeenth century it had only some forty houses, in 1717

about three hundred and fifty, in 1780 more than seven hundred. Cheyne Row has its beautiful houses of the time of Queen Anne intact: and the eighteenth-century cottages, like that in which Turner lived and those in Milman's Street (Nos. 55, 57 and 59), which may be earlier, specially remarked in the Survey of London, Chelsea (Part II), now seem typical of Chelsea in its village rather than palatial aspect. Into that tantalising early history, so exact in many particulars, so scanty in visible remains, there is left an underground avenue of research. At various times, subterranean passages have been excavated, in Beaufort Street, Limerston Street, Paulton's Square, Lower Church Street, Justice Walk, Trafalgar Square, Manresa Road, Oakley Street and Cheyne Walk: though no attempt has apparently ever been made to map out their possible connection. Were they subways leading to the lead conduit which, tradition states, supplied the manor-house with water from Kensington? or themselves channels for water pipes? It is an incidental question why it should have been necessary to bring water from Kensington; but in any case these subways in which is is said a man could walk upright seem too elaborate for their supposed purpose. A fascinating account of one of them is that given by Miss Eliza Gulston (d. 1859) the amateur artist who helped Faulkner with material for his *History of Chelsea*. An old man who had worked as a boy in the "paper manufactory" (i.e. Shrewsbury House) told her of finding a winding stair under a trapdoor in the paper-stainers' room, leading to a passage below. Miss Gulston herself (or the artist who made the drawings, with appended description, now in the Chelsea Public Library) explored and arrived at what was believed to be a Roman guard-house, fronting the river. "The Roman arch prevales all through, which is eliptic." The "further elucidation" for which authorities on Chelsea have hoped has not been forthcoming: though the most recent find was in February 1952 when a lorry sank through the roadway on the bombed area north of the site of Petyt House (school of Queen Anne's time). Beneath was a brick vault, 30 feet long, 8 feet wide, 8 feet high, parallel with the river, the debris on the floor including fragments of eighteenth-century wine bottles and clay pipes. There were signs of a continuation to the west under Old Church Street and north. The bricks, notes the Report of the Chelsea Society, 1952, resembled the seventeenth-century brickwork of the Church. Again, an interesting discovery, though perhaps no more than the foundations of part of old Church Street.

Cheyne Walk

III

GARDENS AND PLEASURES OF
OLD CHELSEA

THE prestige of its healthy air and fertile soil, as well as of its famous early inhabitants, drew people to Chelsea. There is an impressive historical list of invalids and convalescents who went there for health's sake. In 1599 "the gallant Earle of Essex" was reported (by Rowland Whyte) to have "gone to Chelsey where he purposed to be sicke". In 1639 the Earl of Danby came to stay at Danvers House "on account of the malady which assaulted him in old age". Pepys's errant friend, Lord Sandwich, ostensibly at least, came "to take the ayre". Dean Swift, in 1711, wrote to Stella "I design in two days, if possible, to go to lodge at Chelsea for the air, and put myself under the necessity of walking to and from London every day." Dr. John King, who became Rector of Chelsea in 1694 and compiled, between that date and 1712, a MS. "account of the Parish and Rectory" remarked in it that "No village in the vicinity of London contributes more to the ease and recovery of asthmatical and consumptive persons." Shaftesbury gave Chelsea a trial for his asthma.

Not even Chelsea escaped the Plague. Pepys, in April 1666, was put out by finding the White Swan Inn closed because of it. Yet Fanny Burney (or Mme D'Arblay as she was in 1832) then justly said that "Chelsea air is even proverbially salubrious", and on this point the eminent doctors Arbuthnot, Sloane, Mead and others agreed by settling there.

Air and soil by their own happy agreement gave, it seems, a special luxuriance to Chelsea gardens, though a race of keen and able horticulturists must share the credit. The fragrance of herbs drifts to us from the seventeenth century. Evelyn had orange trees from the gardens of Beaufort House. Narcissus Luttrell, the bibliographer and book-collector, who bought the Earl of Shaftesbury's house at Little Chelsea, between 1712 and

1717, cultivated twenty-five varieties of pears in its garden. Faulkner (1810) computed that half the vegetables sold at Covent Garden were raised in Chelsea and the adjoining parishes.

It was natural enough, then, that Chelsea should be the site of what is now the oldest Botanic Garden in the country, left to the Society of Apothecaries in 1673 by Charles Cheyne.

The "Physick", "Botanick", or "Apothecaries'" Garden, still existing, may have lost that peculiar fertility that once was Chelsea's. "The growth of London", lamented Reginald Blunt in 1900 (though even after that date—in 1902—new buildings, including laboratory and lecture-room were put up), "has now encircled it in its grimy toils, and the herbs and exotic plants which it was established to cultivate and study, either will not grow at all, or vegetate reluctantly and without developing their medicinal qualities". The visitor peers through locked gates at the walks, the distant glimmer—sculptural phantom—of Rysbrack's statue of Sir Hans Sloane (14), yet three-quarters of the world's cotton crop are descended from its cotton seeds and it is still a centre of active research.

In its time it has been of great practical use: and in the seventeenth and eighteenth centuries became famous under a series of able men. The botanist John Watts was appointed curator in 1680; a greenhouse was built; an exchange of plants arranged with Dr. Hermann of Leyden in 1682; in 1683 its long celebrated, four cedars of Lebanon were planted. Of these two died in 1771, a third in 1878, the last in 1903, their lasting memorial is the set of four chairs in the Hall of the Society of Apothecaries made from a branch blown down in 1848.

Evelyn approved in 1685, "August 7, I went to see Mr. Watts, Keeper of the Apothecaries' Garden of simples at Chelsea, where there is a collection of innumerable varieties of that sort; particularly, besides many rare annuals, the tree bearing Jesuit's bark, which had done such wonders in quartan agues. What was very ingenious was the subterraneous heat, conveyed by a stove under the conservatory, all vaulted with brick, so as he has the doores and windowes open in the hardest frosts, secluding only the snow." In 1691 the "banks set with shades of herbs in the Irish stitch-way" were much admired; but the Garden gained its highest prestige with the support and interest of Sir Hans Sloane, who bestowed it (1722) on the Apothecaries at a nominal rent, on the sole condition that they should supply fifty dried specimens of plants to the Royal Society yearly. The great Linnaeus, who visited Chelsea in 1736 and collected plants in the garden, highly praised its demonstrators and curators, who remain distinguished in botanical history: Philip Miller, "Prince of Gardeners", author of the *Gardener's Dictionary* (appointed curator, 1722), his successor (in 1771), William Forsyth, William Curtis, author of *Flora Londinensis* (1776)—an account of all plants within ten miles of London—are among them. The names of botanical genera—Milleria, Hudsonia, Forsythia, Randia, Petiveria, Sherardia, preserve the names of those associated with the Physick Garden; the tree "from which the Hottentots and Caffres make their Javelins" was called Curtisia. The organised growth of Kew Gardens from 1795 may be traced back to the experience gained by its manager William Aiton, as assistant to Miller at Chelsea.

The blooms of Chelsea inspired the artist. Elizabeth Blackwell, wife of the wild adventurer Alexander Blackwell (who was eventually executed for political conspiracy in Sweden), raised money to rescue her husband from a debtor's prison by drawing plants in the Physick Garden. With the encouragement of William Rand and Sir Hans Sloane, the lady (who lived in neighbouring Swan Walk—she was buried in the old church in 1758) made engravings of five hundred of the rarest and medically most useful of the plants, coloured them by hand and had them successfully published in 1737 as *A Curious Herbal*. It seems in accord with Chelsea's character that the Dutch flower painter Van Huysum should have lived there two years, in Sir Robert Walpole's house, and that Horace Walpole should mention, in his collection, "a pot of carnations drawn at Chelsea from the life by Van Huysum".

Valetudinarians found a renewed or novel attraction in eighteenth-century Chelsea when an aristocratic Venetian,

14 Sir Hans Sloane

From the statue in the Physic Garden by Rysbrack (1737)

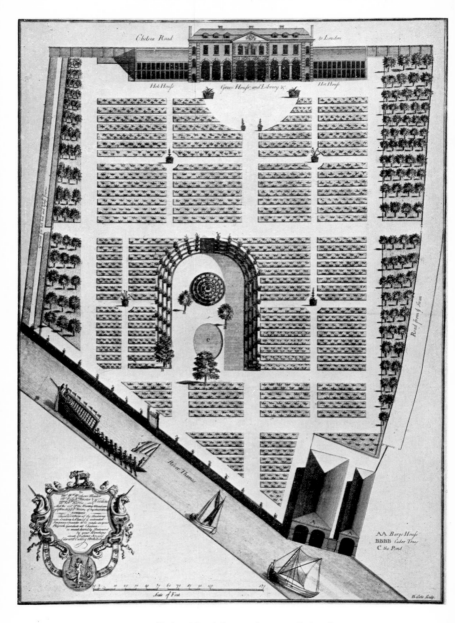

15 "The Physick Garden at Chelsea"

From a print by B. Cole after Edward Oakley's Plan

Dr. Bartholomew Dominiceti, installed his medicated baths at his house in Cheyne Walk (No. 6), which he took in 1765. As an annexe to the house he built what Faulkner describes as an "elegant" brick and wooden building (100 feet by 16 feet) containing the baths and "fumigatory stoves", and "four sweating bed-chambers, to be directed to any degree of heat", the water and vapour being "impregnated with the properties of such herbs and plants as might be supposed most efficacious to the case". Dominiceti claimed to have spent £37,000 on these devices and extensions, of which the Survey of London, Chelsea (Part I) notes in 1909 two remaining rooms, one with "a curious metal-lined recess, the shape of which suggests the reception of a large medicinal bottle of some kind".

It was estimated (by the doctor) that some sixteen thousand people, including Edward, Duke of York, perspired at Cheyne Walk under Dominiceti's care. Sir John Fielding, the blind magistrate and half-brother of the novelist, was all in favour of the treatment and vouched for a number of cures, including that of Miss A—— S——, sister of Lady W—— W——, who suffered from general debility and swelling of the knees but after a course of vapour baths and "saponaceous frictions" was able to get to her coach "with only a thin lady's cane in her hand" and soon "often walked a mile".

Somewhat unfairly Dominiceti has been the object of ridicule. It was his misfortune to be discussed at the table of Dr. Johnson, who observed "there is nothing in all his boasted system". Reasoned argument from one of the company provoked that most famous and unreasonable of his retorts, "Well, sir, go to Dominiceti and get thyself fumigated, but be sure that the steam be directed to the *head* for *that* is the *peccant* part." The great man's antagonist and the Venetian doctor seem equally the butt of the "triumphant roar of laughter" that followed. A species of Turkish bath and a variety of bath salts scarcely deserved it; yet Chelsea historians once spoke with contempt of the "Italian quack" and "charlatan", implacably chronicle his bankruptcy and disappearance in 1782.

A "quack", however, they may have felt, was part of the "fun of the fair" and Chelsea in Dominiceti's time was quite a fair—or pleasure-ground. The pleasant air and rural setting were attractive to many besides invalids. Lovers came out to Chelsea Fields—to quote Gay, early in the century, in his *Epistle to Pulteney*:

> Chelsea's meads o'erhear perfidious vows
> And the press'd grass defrauds the grazing cows.

Places of refreshment were many: the vista of vanished inns as long as that of the palaces; Chelsea, Hawthorne remarked, with an accent of disapproval was "endowed with a prodigious number of pot-houses"; though these, in his time, were the Victorian counterparts of older resorts, the names tenaciously remaining.

The "Queen's Elm", at the Fulham Road end of Church Street, recalls that here Queen Elizabeth was supposed to have sheltered under an elm in the company of Lord Burleigh whom she was visiting at Chelsea: the Queen's tree being mentioned in the Parish Books in 1586, when loyal Chelsea planted a commemorative "arbour" or ring of nine elms, the spot being referred to by Swift in 1711 as the "Nine Elms". The "Cow and Calf (or Calves)", later the "Admiral Keppel", was the old drovers' house, at the eastern corner of Chelsea Common, on the Fulham Road between Keppel Street and Marlborough Road (now Draycott Avenue), adjoining the Pound. Rebuilt as the "Admiral Keppel" in 1790 (according to Alfred Beaver) it stood on the boundary between Chelsea and Kensington, "older inhabitants" Beaver says, in 1892, remembering the custom by which boys, beating the bounds on Ascension Day, went in at the front door and out through a window at the back: while T. C. Croker recalls the legend beneath the sign, before the house was again rebuilt in 1856:

> Stop, brave boys and quench your thirst
> If you won't drink your horses murst.

The "Goat and Boots" at the east corner of Park Walk and Fulham Road preserves the memory of the original, seventeenth-century "Goat" (which had common rights for "2 cows and

68

1 heifer"). Its sign, an emblem ingeniously and doubtfully explained as a corruption of the Dutch "der Goden Boode" (or Messenger of the Gods) denoting a "Mercury" post-house, was supposed to have been painted by George Morland (to pay his bill), and repainted by the tapestry designer Le Blon.

The taverns indeed make a prodigious catalogue of picturesque titles: in the King's Road were the "Man in the Moon", the "Globe", the "World's End" (dubious rendezvous which Mrs. Foresight and Mrs. Frail in Congreve's *Love for Love* detect each other's having visited), the "Six Bells" with its bowling alley: in Church Street, the old "White Horse" (destroyed by fire and rebuilt, 1840) a sixteenth-century timber-framed house, with much carved ornament and projecting brackets in the shape of human figures, and the old "Black Lion" (*c.* 1690); in Lawrence Street, the "Cross Keys", convenient for the pottery workers at the near-by manufactory. In Cheyne Walk, a little west of Oakley Street, was the "Magpye and Stump", a Tudor house (burnt down, 1886) where the Courts Leet and Baron met to fine those who failed to repair the river wall, or let their cattle stray; and a parish feast for the poor was held from Stuart until Victorian times. Here, in a room with a painted ceiling, Colonel Despard hatched his plot to assassinate the King and seize the Tower and Bank of England, for which he was hanged and beheaded in 1803. Most famous of all was the "Old Swan" (demolished after being turned into a brewery, in 1873, to make way for the Chelsea Embankment), on the river's edge with projecting wooden balconies and a terrace and steps to the water. Here Pepys and Mrs. Knipp made merry, while Mrs. Pepys sulked, and gay companies in the eighteenth century watched the finish of the annual waterman's race for Doggett's coat and badge. This institution, founded in 1716 to commemorate the anniversary of George I's accession, by Thomas Doggett (comedian, playwright, theatre manager and Whig), the prize being a coat of the Whig colour, orange, and badge bearing the White Horse of Hanover, remained part of Chelsea's pageantry(16). It incited Thomas Dibdin, when visiting the

"Swan" to nautical opera: and the genial pathos of Tom Tug's lines in *The Waterman* has its local interest:

> Then farewell my trim-built wherry
> Oars and coat and badge farewell,
> Never more at Chelsea ferry
> Shall your Thomas take a spell.

Finally, at the eastern boundary of Chelsea, in the Five Fields, now Pimlico, extending east beyond Chelsea Barracks and the Buckingham Palace Road, were the neighbouring "Star and Garter" and "Dwarf's" taverns. Faulkner locates the "Dwarf's Tavern" "on the spot in Chelsea Fields which was afterwards called Spring Gardens between Ebury Street and Belgrave Terrace". In the eighteenth century, the district was, normally, a lonely marsh, its silence disturbed only by the shots of the duellist, the sportsman after snipe, and, perhaps, of the prowling highwayman. But at holiday times the influx of Londoners created a more cheerful atmosphere. They came to see the famous John Coan, the Norfolk Dwarf, known also as the "Jovial Pigmy", hailed, from the Haymarket stage, as "thou wonder of a Chelsea Field". They devoured the ham, collared eels, potted beef and drank the "sound old bright Wine and Punch like Nectar" which the Dwarf provided for "those that love to live well"; and admired the fireworks at the "Star and Garter" devised by Carlo Genovini, "the Italian artificer from Rome". In 1762 the visiting "Cherokee King and his Two Chiefs" were "greatly pleased" with the curiosities of the "Dwarf's Tavern"; the Guillochees, Tourbilions and Gerbes of the Fire-Work confected by Genovini "in Honour of the last victory gained by the Forces of His Majesty over the French Army in Germany"; and the horsemanship of Mr. Johnson who, "to the great Surprise of the Spectators leaps over the horse when at his greatest Rate". The Cherokee King and his chiefs drank tea with the Jovial Pigmy: and most Chelsea taverns were provided with tea gardens, with rustic arbours and benches (the "World's End" gardens look quite delightful in the old—early nineteenth-century—water-colour in the Chelsea Public Library); also

16   The finish of the race for Doggett's Coat and Badge at the old Swan Inn, Chelsea

From the watercolour by Thomas Rowlandson (1756-1827)

17 "Four Corners. Played at the Swan, Chelsea"
From a Bowles print

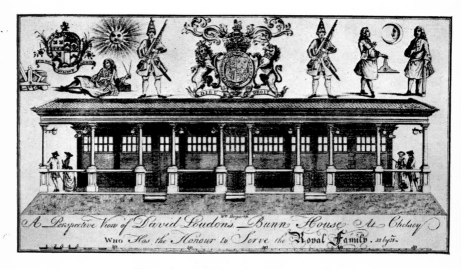

18 "David Loudon's Bunn House at Chelsey"
From a trade card by William Hogarth (c. 1730)

with skittle or bowling alleys, the local game at the old "Swan" being called "Four Corners" and the skittles arranged in diamond formation(17).

Whatever its potations, the eighteenth century could be very lively on tea and buns: and the old Bunn House was an immensely popular resort(18). It would be a quibble to say that this early eighteenth-century establishment (pulled down in 1839) which stood at the end of Jew's Row (Pimlico Road) not far from Grosvenor Row, was over the Chelsea border. The bun belonged to Chelsea. Swift, in the *Journal to Stella*, 1712, renders the street-cry "r-r-r-r-rare Chelsea Buns", remarks on the crowd of "boys and wenches buzzing about the cake-shops like fairs"; on the "great cakes frothed with sugar and decorated with streamers of tinsel". Beneath the colonnade of the Bunn House, even Royalty nibbled the "flour of the ovens! a zephyr in paste" (in the words of a local versifier whom Alfred Beaver quotes but does not name). George II was a customer, and George III and his Queen and all the Princes and Princesses. The populace followed. In the early nineteenth century, according to George Bryan (author of *Chelsea in the Olden and Present Times*), at least 240,000 buns were sold on Good Friday, and some 200,000 people collected, in what was "a fair to all intents and purposes". It is quite in accord with the Chelsea sense of tradition that the Bunn House should have been revived, in Sloane Square, in the Festival summer of 1951, when it was once more a great attraction.

It was, perhaps, the fame of Sir Hans Sloane's collection, that caused such places of entertainment to collect and exhibit curious objects—among which even the proprietors could be numbered. At the Bunn House, the visitor would examine; the half-gallon silver mug, given by George III; the lead soldiers, British Grenadiers of 1745, presenting arms, four feet high; the portrait of "Aurungzabe, Emperor of Persia"; the paper model of St. Mary Redcliffe; the model of the Bunn House itself, with moving figures; find also a curious interest in the last proprietor, Mr. Hand (the Bunn House had supported four generations of Hands)—once an officer in the Staffordshire Militia and known as "Captain Bun"—in his long dressing-gown and Turkish fez.

A like curious interest attaches to James Salter ("Don Saltero") and his tavern-cum-museum known as Don Saltero's Coffee House. Salter, an Irishman, who had been a servant of Sir Hans Sloane and accompanied him on his travels, was decidedly a character, one of those with a gift for attracting facetious praise. Steele in No. 34 of *The Tatler*, 1708, set the style in his well-known description of this "Sage of thin and meagre countenance ... of that sect which the ancients called Gingivistae—in our language tooth-drawers. . . . My love of mankind made one very benevolent to Mr. Salter; for such is the name of this eminent barber and antiquary . . ."

It was one of his patrons, Vice-Admiral Munden, who with a flash of humorous invention, christened him "Don Saltero", suggesting at once a Chelsea Quixote—and buccaneer. The flavour tinges Salter's own doggerel verse in the *Weekly Journal*, June 23, 1723:

> Sir, fifty years since to Chelsea great,
> From Rodman on the Irish main,
> I strolled . . .

He was in Chelsea in 1685, for he was fined £6 in that year by the Court Leet, for allowing the adjacent section of river wall to decay. Moving from "Lombard Street", he can be traced as a "coffeeman" in Church Row and Danvers Street (and to this period Steele's description refers), but his palmy days came when he moved in 1718 to one of the new houses (No. 18) just built in Cheyne Walk. The house has been so much altered that little of its original character now remains, though a neatly lettered plate at the front gate, "Don Saltero's", bears its own witness to the persistence of Chelsea legend.

It was the meeting-place of local celebrities, and of visitors from London and elsewhere—Benjamin Franklin came to see Don Saltero's curiosities as well as "the College". The proprietor judiciously joined in the laughter excited by his collection, complacently describing it as a "Knackatory" and himself a "gimcrack-whim" collector. It consisted, no doubt, in part of throw-outs from Sir Hans Sloane's museum; like the "lignified hog"—a tree-root of curious shape—Benjamin Franklin's asbestos purse; and many "corals, chrystals, ores, shells . . . stuffed animals . . . idols . . . missals . . . butterflies, medals, models, fire-arms, fishes . . .", but such items (if Steele did not make them up) as "Pontius Pilate's wife's chambermaid's sister's hat", would seem to have made it a caricature of Sir Hans's serious passion.

Yet so poetic or imaginative is the list of Don Saltero's curiosi-ties that it deserves a somewhat extended enumeration. It includes; the heads of the four Evangelists carved on cherry-stones; a rose of Jericho and an Israelitish shekel; a large worm that eats into the keel of ships in the West Indies; the bark of a tree which when drawn out appears like fine lace; a fairy's or elf's arrow; a piece of Solomon's temple; Job's tears that grow on a tree, wherewith they make anodyne necklaces; the caul of an elephant; a Muscovy snuff-box made of an elk's hoof; a set of beads made of the bones of St. Anthony of Padua; a curious piece of metal found in the ruins of Troy; a starved cat found between the walls of Westminster Abbey when the east end was repaired; a frog, fifteen inches long, found in the Isle of Dogs; the Staffordshire almanack used when the Danes were in England; the lance of Captain Tow-How-Sham, King of the Darien Indians, with which he killed six Spaniards; a cockatrice; Mary, Queen of Scots' pin-cushion; a purse made of a spider from Antigua; and among other animal oddities the "wild man of the woods". There were some who considered Sir Hans Sloane's collection to be no less fantastic and Young, in his *Love of Fame* remarks:

> How his eyes languish! how his thoughts adore
> That painted coat which Joseph *never* wore!
> He shows on holidays, a sacred pin,
> That touch'd the ruff that touch'd Queen Bess's chin.

The famous Coffee House lingered on after the "Don's" death, until 1799 when the collection was sold for £50 and then as a public-house until 1867—an old photograph showing it in this latter phase with charming, small paned, ground-floor

Ranelagh: The Rotunda

windows and two massive lanterns flanking the entrance. Yet the bun and coffee house, the taverns and tea-gardens, were minor attractions when compared with the Rotunda and pleasure grounds of Ranelagh(19).

It was a vulgarisation of the private splendour of Ranelagh House and Gardens. The means by which Richard Jones, third Viscount and first Earl of Ranelagh, attained his fortune were dubious enough to cause his expulsion from the office of Paymaster-General to the Forces, yet before this happened he had been able to build his handsome house adjoining the Hospital and, on the plea of having suffered heavy losses, to secure twenty-three acres with the house for an annual rent to the Hospital of £5. The gardens "curiously kept and elegantly designed" were, in 1705, esteemed the best in England. The great party given for George I by the Earl's daughter in 1715, showed how well gardens and river combined to make a splendid occasion. In 1733 the property was sold to the lessee of Drury Lane, Lacy, who proposed to make it a place of public entertainment. The scheme, costly, and objected to by the Hospital authorities, languished, until a new company, encouraged by the success of Vauxhall Gardens, pushed it through. The Rotunda, in the Ranelagh grounds, built by William Jones, architect to the East

India Company, after the style of the Pantheon in Rome, was opened with a public breakfast in 1742.

Externally, this round building with its sixty windows must have had a faint resemblance to the Albert Hall and internally, as much to the Reading Room of the British Museum as the Pantheon, but its size (internal diameter, 150 feet), its circle of fifty-two boxes (each with its "droll painting" and bell-lamp with candles), its chandeliers suspended from the olive-green ceiling, its grand central fire-place with four black pillars, long provoked wonder rather than architectural comparison.

The splendour, of this "illustrious monument", as one writer termed it, of Mr. Jones's "genius and fancy" was illusionary; an element of burlesque, and perhaps of what is known as *l'ironie anglaise*, tempered the grandiose with the homely and the non-descript. The fact could not be disguised that the core of its magnificence was a series of kitchen ranges. "The enchanted palace of a genie", as Miss Lydia Melford calls it in *Humphry Clinker,* dispensed tea, coffee and bread-and-butter at half a crown a head. "The pomp and splendour of a Roman amphi-theatre", remarked a visitor in 1742, "are devoted to no better use than a twelvepenny entertainment of cold ham and chicken." The subsidiary buildings, the Temple of Pan at the bottom of the garden, the pavilion in the ornamental "canal", sometimes referred to as the "Chinese House" and sometimes as the "Venetian Temple", were pinchbeck. In its off-moments, at various times in its history, it caused disappointment. "I was there last night," says Horace Walpole, shortly after the opening, "but did not find the joy of it. Vauxhall is a little better . . ." A French visitor coldly criticised it as "the most insipid place of amusement one could imagine". Samuel Rogers (1786) describes a grimly frozen moment when it was "so orderly and still you could hear the swishing sound of the ladies' trains". Yet the hypnotic influence of size, fashionable crowds and fireworks, regatta and masquerade, produced, in the main, extravagant superlatives of praise. Walpole changed his tune. "Nobody goes anywhere else—everybody goes there. My lord Chesterfield is so fond of it that he says he has ordered all his letters to be directed thither."

"The floor", he said, ecstatically, "is of beaten princes." To Dr. Johnson, who was fond of these "innocent places of recreation" and went to Ranelagh, as to Vauxhall, with Boswell and company, the *coup d'œil* was the finest thing he had ever seen.

It is interesting to observe the conquest of a not very impressionable German traveller, Carl Philipp Moritz (*Travels in England*, 1782). He paid his entrance and found himself in "a poor, meanlooking and illlighted garden": had some difficulty in getting rid of a familiar young woman who took his arm; and then . . . "suddenly entered a round building, illuminated by many hundred lamps the splendour and beauty of which surpassed anything of the kind I had ever seen before". In this "magic rotondo", the *beau monde* of London "moved perpetually around".

Special performances contributed to its sixty years of success. In 1763 the company was diverted by Bonnell Thornton's burlesque *Ode on St. Cecilia's Day* with "antient British music"— salt box, Jew's Harp, marrow bones and cleavers and "humstrum" or hurdygurdy. In the following year Mozart, aged eight, played on harpsichord and organ. 1769 saw the performance of Dibdin's *Ephesian Matron*. The masquerades were already in the spirit of the Chelsea Arts Ball. Walpole describes in sprightly style, the Jubilee Masquerade of 1749 "after the Venetian manner", with its masked peasants dancing round the Maypole to the sound of tabour and pipe; huntsmen with French horns; troups of harlequins and scaramouches; masked shopkeepers with stalls of china; festoons of flowers hanging from tree to tree . . . Shortly after, the "Subscription Masquerade"; the King disguised in "an old fashioned English habit", the corpulent Duke of Cumberland, in similar dress, looking "like *Cacafoco*, the drunken captain, in *Rule a Wife and Have a Wife*", Miss Pitt with a red veil "which made her look gloriously handsome". Miss Chudleigh was Iphigenia "and so lightly clad that you would have taken her for Andromeda . . . The maids of honour were so offended they would not speak to her . . ." Lady Betty Smithson "had such a pyramid of baubles on her head that she was exactly the Princess of Babylon in Grammont".

A certain licence accompanied what the eighteenth-century memoirist, Mrs. Carter, described as "these revels of Comus". The masquerades were eventually suppressed by the Justices of Middlesex, though the entertainments went on. At the Regatta and Ball of 1775 (the ticket for which was designed by Cipriani and Bartolozzi) the Thames was "a floating town", the guests landing at the stairs at 9 p.m., were met by dazzling clusters of lamps, an orchestra of two hundred and forty musical masters; danced, among imported palm-trees, and in the Temple of Pan. In 1789 Mr. Callot's firework coruscated while the fire-music composed by Mr. Handel was played. In 1792 the view of Mount Etna "painted by Signor Marinari", erupted with a resounding explosion. In 1802 M. Garnerin and Captain Snowden soared up from the gardens in their balloon, landing at Colchester an hour later. In 1803, at a gala given by the Spanish Ambassador, the boxes of the Rotunda became a "Spanish camp", each tent guarded by a boy in Spanish uniform, the gallery was a Temple of Flora, women wreathed with flowers made tea, a Spanish dance was performed by children, "a hundred valets in scarlet and gold, and as many footmen, in sky-blue and silver, waited on the company".

The decline of Ranelagh was swift. By 1805 it had had its day. The decoys sent out, to mingle in fashionable assemblies for the purpose of being overheard remarking "What charming weather for Ranelagh" had lost their power of suggestion. Robert Bloomfield, the "peasant poet" bleakly described the disillusion of the promenade.

> First we trac'd the gay circle all round
> Ay—and then we went round it again.

A new Marius among the ruins of Carthage, Sir Richard Phillips (*Walk from London to Kew*) mourned the demolition (1805) of the Rotunda. He walked along the avenue of trees he had often seen blocked with carriages. "On a spot covered with nettles, thistles and other rank weeds" he met a working man who told him this was the site. Sadly he looked at the broken arches of the cellars "once filled with the choicest wines", traced

the position of the orchestra. The Byfield organ had gone to
Tetbury Church. The melodious falsetto of Tenducci was but
a memory. "All was death-like stillness! Is such, I exclaimed,
the end of human splendour?"

Yet Ranelagh amply remains in the literature of fact and
fiction; especially in the descriptions of Walpole and Smollett,
and Dr. Johnson's remark is classic that there was "half-a-guinea's
worth of inferiority to other people in not having seen it". A
second Ranelagh sprang up in the suburbs of Paris, survived
the Revolution, and lingered until the fortifications of Paris
cut through its gardens in 1840. In Chelsea itself it had its
successor in Cremorne(20, 21).

The beautiful name conjures up a golden rocket in the blue
twilight of a Whistler canvas, the gardens of Cremorne flourished
in the latter half of the nineteenth century, though never so
fashionable as Ranelagh had been. They stood on the site of the
house known as "Chelsea Farm", built by Theophilus, Earl of
Huntingdon, in 1745, the White House, Chelsea, of Girtin's
water-colour, acquired in 1778 by Thomas Dawson, Baron
Dartrey (created Viscount Cremorne in 1785). He employed
James Wyatt to enlarge and improve it. It is described as a
brick house, on the architecture of which nineteenth-century
comment is slighting: but it overlooked the river from which
it was separated by a lawn, with noble elms, ash and oaks.
Philadelphia Hannah, Lady Cremorne, great-grand-daughter
of William Penn, and born in Philadelphia, lived in the house
(her husband died in 1813) until 1825. She left it to her cousin,
Granville Penn, who after several unsuccessful attempts to sell
it, found a buyer in 1831, Charles Random de Bérenger, Baron
de Beaufain. The Baron turned it into a "National Club" for
"various skilful and manly exercises"—they included swimming,
rowing, shooting, fencing, archery, riding, driving, skating,
coursing, hunting and racing—called "The Stadium".

The Stadium (which gave its name to Stadium Street) lasted
until 1841, but did not, apparently, pay its way and was re-opened
as Cremorne Gardens in 1845. Its programme included the
concerts, fireworks, balloon ascents and galas that had made

19 Ranelagh: The interior of the Rotunda, in 1754

From the painting by Antonio Canaletto

20, 21   CREMORNE GARDENS

Both from watercolours by T. Hosmer Shepherd

Ranelagh's success: but, 1845 was not 1745. The cocked hat and French wig were replaced not only by the top hat but by the proletarian cap. The neighbouring public-house was enlarged for the benefit of a rougher element, not content to promenade and drink tea. Beaver speaks of "some years of disreputable existence" before Cremorne was closed as a nuisance to the neighbourhood in 1875. Yet the more garish glitter of its coloured lamps, its theatre and its grottoes, its fountain with the plaster figure of the "Stooping Venus", still have a glamour of their own in retrospect; partly, no doubt, because, in its later days Cremorne was frequented by Whistler and his boatman-artist follower, Walter Greaves, and both have left us romantic pictures of it. The balloon ascent here and in "the Lots" and adjoining grounds of the old Ashburnham House (built for Dr. Benjamin Hoadley in 1745), was a popular item in the sixties of which the "Balloon Tavern", at the angle of Lots Road preserved the memory. There being as yet no gas in Chelsea, the Cremorne Balloon was taken to the Gas Works at Vauxhall—Greaves has drawn its journey back in tow of one of the Citizen Steamboats. It is a "Space Ship" now that one sees from Chelsea, in the present-day Festival Gardens! Though they are across the water in Battersea it is appropriate that the same stretch of river as of old should border the modern pleasure ground.

Richard Hand
the Oldest Original Chelsey Bunn Baker
at the *Kings Arms* at *Chelsey*
Remov'd from y⁰ Old Original Chelsey Bunn house
N.B. Who has the Honour to Serve the
Royal Family

Richard Hand's Trade Card (1718)

83

IV

THE WRITER'S CHELSEA

THE Chelsea of the fashionable and pleasure-seeking, became also, in the eighteenth century, the resort of an increasing number of people of ideas and talent. Politically it might be called Whig, in view of the presence of such recipients of Whig patronage as Addison and Steele, and in the early Hanoverian days of Sir Robert Walpole himself. In science, it could claim (over a longer period) by residence or association, six Presidents of the Royal Society, the Earl of Carberry, Robert Boyle, Sir Joseph Banks, Sir Isaac Newton, Sir Christopher Wren, Sir Hans Sloane. It had its distinguished doctors and botanists, and already a certain number of artists. Men of letters, to whom the attractions of local good company and easy access to town were as obvious as to others, above all found it a quiet and pleasant place to write in.

"We dined", says Swift, in the *Journal to Stella* (September, 1710), "at a country-house near Chelsea where Mr. Addison often retires." The country house has been identified with Sandford Manor, Sandy End, Fulham, the reputed home of Nell Gwynn (surviving into the twentieth century but marooned among gas works). It seems likely that Addison occupied it at intervals until 1716, when he married Sarah, Countess of Warwick; that some, at least, of his essays for the *Tatler* (1709–11) and *Spectator* (1711–14) were written there, that he would find it an agreeable diversion to walk across the fields to see his Countess at Holland House, Kensington (where he died in 1719). That he mused on the history of Chelsea's first great man is shown by references in the *Spectator* to Sir Thomas More. "I shall only observe", said Addison, "that what was philosophy in this extraordinary man would be phrenzy in anyone who does not resemble him, as well in the cheerfulness of his temper, as in the sanctity of his life and manners." The urbanity of the Humanist appealed to the Augustan. If More had been simply a martyr, Addison would have been colder.

While Addison was at Sandy End, his collaborator, the original Tatler, Richard Steele(26) who "fared [with Addison] like a distressed prince who calls in a powerful neighbour . . . I could not subsist without dependence on him", was living at Cheyne Walk, i.e. renting a house at the water-side, rated at £14 a year. The sociability of the easy-going Anglo-Irishman, which caused him to delight in all places of public resort, led him to describe Don Saltero's as zestfully as White's Chocolate House, Will's Coffee House, the "Grecian" or St. James's. One guesses at a convivial occasion in the letter he wrote from Chelsea, in 1716, to his wife: "Mr. Fuller and I came hither to dine in the air, but the maid has been so slow that we are benighted, and chuse to lie here than go this road in the dark. I lie at our own house, and my friend at a relation's in the town."

Steele was then in expansive mood; in favour, as a Whig stalwart, with George I, who had knighted him the year before; the manager of Drury Lane with a handsome share of the profits, but the prospect was soon to darken. His "dear Prue" died in 1718, a breach with Addison remained open, until the latter's death in 1719. Debts mounted up; Drury Lane passed into other hands; after a few years he vanished into Wales, and London and Chelsea knew him no more.

Neither Addison nor Steele ever seems so alertly and vividly present in Chelsea as Jonathan Swift. A middle-aged Irish parson, with a mission from the Irish Archbishops to secure concessions for the Church in Ireland, he had no specific attachment to place—or party—in London. He came to Chelsea in 1711, perhaps because it was the resort of his Whig friends, Addison and Steele; though by then, in his efforts to gain remit-tance of the tax ("First Fruits") on Irish benefices, he was veering to the Tory side temporarily in the ascendant: and Chelsea comes frequently into his famous journal—letters to his "star", Esther Johnson.

He lodged in Church Lane (Church Street). "I got here in the stage-coach with Patrick and my portmantua [*sic*] for sixpence, and pay six shilling a week for one silly room with confounded coarse sheets." It may not have been without its political signifi- cance that the lodging was "over against Dr. Atterbury's house". "And yet, perhaps," Swift remarks in his sharp and casual style, "I shall not like the place the better for that." But the Jacobite Dr. Atterbury's Toryism was in accord with Swift's change of political front, and the Doctor no doubt saw him as a possible ally. Mrs. Atterbury sent over veal, small beer and ale: and subsequently Swift's dinners with her husband are often mentioned.

His view of Chelsea was vivid rather than affectionate. It was the critical foreigner who remarked on the "r-r-r-r-rare Chelsea Buns". "I bought one to-day in my walk; it cost me a penny; it was stale and I did not like it": who called Chelsea's "haymaking nymphs" "perfect drabs": who, on a rainy day found "the cunning natives of Chelsea have outwitted me, and taken up all the three stage-coaches": it was the merciless man of intellect who called the Earl of Ranelagh "the vainest old fool that ever I saw": who, in the *Tatler* satirised Mary Astell of the "Serious Call". *Gulliver's Travels* was still in the future; Swift's powers, in his short Chelsea period, in revenge for Whig apathy towards the claims of the Irish church, were being diverted to masterly political journalism on behalf of the Tory cause. He went often to London for parleys with Harley and Bolingbroke: and walked back "up the Pall Mall, through the Park, out at Buckingham House, and so to Chelsea a little beyond the church". It took him "something less than an hour: it is two good miles, and just five thousand seven hundred and forty-eight steps".

"I had no money to lose": thus he concisely explains the reason for walking, at any hour, and in spite of the dangers of the road. One sees the grim figure striding through the Five Fields at one in the morning counting his paces, careless of highwaymen and footpads, with all the sense of immunity that his cloth, his genius and his empty purse could give. Once he and his servant Patrick interfered in a brawl between a drunken parson and a seaman. The seaman followed them to Chelsea, cursing. "A pretty scene for one that just came from sitting with the prime

22   Carlyle's House:
No. 24 Cheyne Row

23   Leigh Hunt's House:
No. 22 Upper Cheyne Row

24   Rossetti's House:
No. 16 Cheyne Walk

25   No. 30 Cheyne Row

26   Sir Richard Steele
From a portrait by Sir Godfrey Kneller

27   Tobias Smollett
From a portrait by an unknown Italian artist

28   Leigh Hunt
*From a portrait by
Samuel Lawrence*

ministers: I had no money in my pocket and so could not be robbed." When it rained or was very hot, he went to London by water (he grumbles because there were no boats on Sunday): and in the hot June of 1711, he swam in the Thames at Chelsea, with all the ceremony of the period, borrowing a napkin from his landlady for a cap, while Patrick attended holding his nightgown, shirt and slippers. He left Chelsea in the following month, expressing on that account neither satisfaction nor regret.

The literary annals of Chelsea in the Augustan age of Queen Anne might be extended to include Thomas Shadwell, playwright and poet laureate, remembered less for his *Squire of Alsatia* than as the victim of Dryden's *Mac Flecknoe*:

> The rest to some faint meaning make pretence
> But Shadwell never deviates into sense.

Shadwell died in Chelsea, 1692. His son, Sir John Shadwell, physician to Queen Anne, took a house there from Dr. John Arbuthnot, also a physician but more celebrated for lively satire, like that of his *History of John Bull* (1712), and in Swift's view "better at his art than his trade". John Gay certainly knew Chelsea and may have lived there for a while, before 1714—when he fell out of favour with the Duchess of Monmouth—as her secretary at Monmouth House (the old Lawrence House). It is in Monmouth House, turned, after the Duchess's death in 1732, into two dwellings, that we take up a later thread of literary history. In one of them there settled, in 1753, a peppery, Scottish ex-naval surgeon, turned writer—Tobias Smollett.

Smollett(27) came to Chelsea, as so many had done "for the air", hoping it would benefit his young and delicate daughter, an only child. In this, and in most other ways during his ten years' stay, he was disappointed. His daughter died of tuberculosis at Monmouth House in 1763, when she was fifteen. Her death caused him to leave and try to forget his sorrow in those travels through France and Italy of which he wrote a somewhat peevishly critical account.

In the meantime, his work and fortunes did not prosper. Before Chelsea he had been unsuccessful as a doctor in London and Bath. On the other hand he had written two first-rate novels, *Roderick Random* and *Peregrine Pickle*: but now he committed himself to a dreary programme of hackwork, his much-criticised *History of England* being a sad example. An attack in the *Critical Review* on Admiral Knowles—a commander at Carthagena where Smollett saw action—earned him a fine of £100 and three months imprisonment for libel—the period he occupied in writing his worst novel in improbable imitation of *Don Quixote, Sir Lancelot Greaves*. Prison varied a life in Chelsea, spent, he says, "in the shade of obscurity, neglecting and neglected". Yet he had kindly memories of the place. "I cannot help respecting Chelsea as a second native place", he wrote to a friend from Boulogne, in August 1763, "notwithstanding the irreparable misfortunes which happened to me while I resided in it."

His isolation in Chelsea was from fashionable society ("I have not spoken to a nobleman for some years"). For this his temper, generous but cantankerous, seems to have been to blame. Distinguished or powerful friends, like Garrick and Wilkes, visited him until he invited enmity by fierce invective against them. He spent his "vacant hours among a set of honest, phlegmatic Englishmen, whom I cultivate for their integrity of heart and simplicity of manners". They were, no doubt, his "brotherhood" of the "Swan", and frequenters of Don Saltero's, ex-officers, like Captain Robert Mann, "my neighbour in Chelsea" and "club companion these seven long years", and the "unfortunate brothers of the quill" whom he treated on Sundays, to beef, pudding, port, punch and Calvert's entire butt-beer.

Leaving Chelsea, he did not forget it; his last and best novel *Humphry Clinker* refers entertainingly to it, though written after seven years absence, in his final retirement at a cottage near Leghorn. Carlyle in 1834 was near enough to Lawrence Street to "shoot a gun into Smollett's old house (at this very time getting pulled down)"; added the briskly garbled description "where he wrote 'Count Fathom' and was wont every Saturday to dine a company of hungry authors and set them fighting together".

At the beginning of the nineteenth century Chelsea found an admirable historian in Thomas Faulkner, bookseller and printer, whose shop was at No. 1 Paradise Row, on the site later occupied by the "Chelsea Pensioner" public-house. Born in 1777, he was a member of that race of antiquarians who were giving a new perspective to English architecture and history. He began writing as a contributor to the *Gentleman's Magazine*, produced his *Short Account of Chelsea Hospital* when he was twenty-eight and the first edition of his *History of Chelsea* five years later, then, at intervals, Histories of Fulham, Hammersmith, Kensington and Brentford, Chiswick and Ealing. He lived to be seventy-eight, died in Smith Street in 1855 and was buried in Brompton Cemetery. It is pleasant to think of such an essentially local person, surrounded by dusty folios, looking absent-mindedly up at a customer from some ancient volume, poring with insatiable interest over the lists of Baptisms, Marriages and Burials in the Parish Register, the minutest details of family record. He was capable of prefacing an account of Chelsea Manor with a history of the feudal system, though his leisurely approach has a period charm. He was inaccurate in his copies of epitaphs in the church, yet he did go to original sources. He scrutinised the finances of the parish workhouse with the closeness of an accountant; but if some small particulars bulked too large, many more were of value. After contemplating his modest industry with due respect we come once again into the mainstream of literature in considering the Chelsea of Thomas Carlyle(30).

It was indeed Carlyle's Chelsea, in so masterful a fashion did he survey and appropriate it as his special domain. He came, like so many settlers, in early middle-life, in the year 1834, that is, when he was thirty-nine. He was nine years married—to the daughter of a Dumfriesshire doctor, Jane Baillie Welsh, who disappointed in her love for Edward Irving, the friend of Carlyle, had accepted him after considerable doubt and wavering. For six years they had lived on the small estate she inherited at Craigenputtock, not far from Dumfries. There was the silence there, by which he always set so much store, broken only by the bleating of sheep on the lonely grasslands between the house and the Solway Hills: but too much silence, even for him, absorbed in the production of reviews and essays, his history of German literature, the philosophy of *Sartor Resartus*. With a typical relish of the worst side of things, he called it "the dreariest spot in all the British dominions". The silence was certainly too much for the sociable Jane Welsh. It was a relief for both of them when, with £200 at his command, he obeyed Jeffrey's injunction to "bring your blooming Eve out of your blasted Paradise" and in June 1834 they set up house in London at No. 5 (now No. 24) Cheyne Row(22).

Quite apart from philosophy, Carlyle had a wonderful gift of observing and recording his observation, and his first impressions, less critical than usual, make one intensely feel what he saw. He gave a picture, that was both like and unlike the old Chelsea, a nineteenth-century view, that is, of the eighteenth-century scene. The social ambience was altered. Cheyne Row was no longer a minor, aristocratic elegance but "a genteel neighbourhood, two old ladies on one side, unknown character on the other, but with 'pianos'". Modern sympathy with Queen Anne and Georgian architecture is so intimate that examples still seem modern with that modernity of which the eighteenth century so much approved: but this quality is blurred by the focus of Carlyle's vision. His description of Cheyne Row "flag-pathed, sunk storied [i.e. with basements], iron-railed ... all old-fashioned and tightly done up" is tinged with the spirit and style of a romantic period. The house was aged, massive and rambling to his eyes: "antique, wainscoted to the very ceiling", the balustrade "massive ... (in the old style)", "the floors thick as a rock, wood of them, here and there worm-eaten, yet capable of cleanliness ..." the presses and shelved closets "queer" and "old". He exaggerated the capacity of the "china-room or pantry, or I know not what ... fit to hold crockery for the whole street", the places "to hang, say, three dozen hats or cloaks in", the "many crevices". On the whole he approved the "roomy and sufficient" house, and the rent of £35 a year.

As to the surroundings, something, perhaps, of uncongenial formality in the "tree avenues, once a bishop's pleasure-grounds" beyond the garden, caused him to describe the view as "un-picturesque but rather cheerful". On the other hand, "Our row, which for the last three doors or so is a street, and none of the noblest, runs out upon a 'Parade' (perhaps they call it) running along the shore of the river, a broad highway with huge, shady trees, boats lying moored and a smell of shipping and tar." The verbal Dutch picture merges into an early-Victorian print in words. Its placidity is disturbed by "white-trowsered, white-shirted Cockneys dashing by like arrows in their long canoes of boats; beyond the green, beautiful knolls of Surrey . . . a most artificial green-painted yet lively, fresh, almost operatic-looking business".

There was no doubt he liked Chelsea from the first. His remark that it was "a singular heterogeneous kind of spot, very dirty and confused in some places, quite beautiful in others" was without rancour and portended reluctant affection. He remembered in later years the London journey to Cheyne Row, in a hackney coach with his wife and the canary "Chico" she had brought from Craigenputtock; "the cheerful gipsy life we had among the litter and the carpenters for three incipient days": and there was a literary neighbour "in the next street"—Leigh Hunt(28).

Leigh Hunt, too, had recently moved, with his wife and seven children, "from the noise and dust of the New Road", to "a corner in Chelsea", No. 4 (now No. 22) Upper Cheyne Row(23). He was a struggling writer of fifty, whose more exciting personal experiences, his friendship with Shelley and Byron, his residence in Italy with "my noble friend", were already behind him. He, too, had his description of his new address, though more gently framed than that of Carlyle and more receptive to the spirit of the eighteenth century, from which, in date, he was not so far removed. He used the same adjective as Carlyle "old-fashioned", but identifying himself with it:

The house was of that old-fashioned sort which I have always loved best, familiar to the eyes of my parents, and associated with childhood. It had seats in the windows, a small third room on the first floor, of which I made a *sanctum* . . . and there were a few lime trees in front, which in their due season diffused a fragrance.

That riverward Chelsea was quiet then, in the eighteen-thirties, no present-day visitor would doubt. It was a quietude beautifully analysed in Hunt's *Autobiography*. "A little back-room in a street in London is farther removed from the noise than the front-room in a country town." In Chelsea this sudden remoteness conveyed the delightful feeling of being "at the end of the world". "The air of the neighbouring river was so re-freshing and the quiet of the 'no-thoroughfare' so full of repose that although our fortunes were at their worst, and my health almost of a piece with them, I felt for some weeks as if I could sit still for ever, embalmed in silence." Carlyle was to blame the street cries and crowing Chelsea cocks for an infinity of dyspeptic and neurotic torture. More placid in temperament and better in digestion, Leigh Hunt found in these noises the gentlest accompaniment and accentuation of stillness; in the cries of street vendors, a timbre different from that "in other quarters of the suburbs"—the "quaintness and melodiousness which procured them the reputation of having been composed by Purcell and others". There was, he says, "an old seller of fish, in particular, whose cry of 'shrimps as large as prawns,' was such a regular, long-drawn, and truly pleasing melody, that in spite of his hoarse and, I am afraid, drunken voice, I used to wish for it of an evening, and hail it when it came".

In those "old-fashioned", panelled rooms of Cheyne Row, the two men subjected each other, each to his own variety of searching examination. It is curious that, on the whole, Carlyle should have liked Hunt, curious, that is, because Hunt was so much a being of another world and company, for whose intimates, Shelley and Charles Lamb, Carlyle reserved the fiercest and nastiest of his remarks. "A good man" is the summing up in Carlyle's *Journal* of September 8, 1834: though this goodness was to be differentiated from a mode of life that was by no means to be admired and the light, polished manner of an earlier age that Carlyle found it hard to understand and could only describe as "idle" ("free, cheery, *idly* melodious as bird on bough").

Yet the description of Hunt, visiting No. 5 Cheyne Row, talking amiably to his Scottish hosts, listening with every sign of pleasure to Jane Welsh's old Scotch tunes on the piano, bending graciously over the frugal morsel of porridge which he found "endlessly admirable", is Carlyle at his most, and even most comically, effective. How well he calls up the "fine, clean, elastic figure", leaning on the mantelpiece "'as if I were a *Lar*', said he once, 'or permanent Household God here!' (such his polite *Ariel*-like way)", or taking leave with the words "(voice very fine) as if in sport of parody: While I to sulphurous and penal fire . . ." In Upper Cheyne Row, however, the Victorian energy of words seemed intended with more, if unconscious, cruelty, to pin the Regency butterfly—if such a term can be applied to as hard-working a person as Leigh Hunt. His house, said Carlyle, "excels all you have ever read of—a poetical Tinker-dom, without parallel even in literature"—already Carlyle foreshadows the attitude of Dickens to Mr. Skimpole in *Bleak House*. "In his family room where are a sickly large wife and a whole school of well-conditioned wild children, you will find half-a-dozen old rickety chairs gathered from half-a-dozen different hucksters and all seeming engaged, and just pausing, in a violent hornpipe. On these and around them and over the dusty table and ragged carpet lie all kinds of litter—books, papers, egg-shells, scissors and last night when I was there, the torn heart of a quartern loaf." In these surroundings and sat on a window-sill, in his printed dressing-gown, Hunt would engage on "the liveliest dialogue on philosophy and the prospects of man (who is to be beyond measure happy yet)".

To Carlyle the household disclosed "hugger-mugger, *un*thrift and sordid collapse"—he says nothing of Hunt's industry, knew nothing of the expense of seven children and was not immune from the fear of contamination by failure. The "hugger-mugger" had "to be associated with on cautious terms". Yet, while he pitied, Carlyle was aware that his neighbour was repelled by what "he would call 'Scotch', 'Presbyterian', who knows what", qualities in Carlyle and his wife which he himself preferred to describe as "something of positive, of practically steadfast". He may have been mistaken. In Hunt's expressed view, Carlyle was "one of the kindest and best, as well as most eloquent of men": but not immune from criticism. "Mr. Carlyle sees that there is a good deal of rough work in the operations of nature; he seems to think himself bound to consider a good deal of it devilish, after the old Covenanter fashion, in order that he may find something angelical in giving it the proper quantity of vituperation and blows . . ." His "antipathy to 'shams' is highly estimable and salutary . . . But the danger of the habit of denouncing—of looking at things from the antipathetic instead of the sympathetic side—is that a man gets such a love for the pleasure and exaltation of fault-finding, as tempts him, in spite of himself, to make what he finds . . ." Save for a passing glimpse, the Hunts quickly vanished from the Carlyles' ken. Struggling with his casual journalism, London essays, his anti-war poem *Captain Sword and Captain Pen*, his unsuccessful drama *A Legend of Florence*, Leigh Hunt remained in Chelsea for seven years, though except in his *Autobiography* he has left no account of the district. With his wife and family, he moved in 1840 to Kensington and "although my health was not bettered, as I hoped it would have been by the change, but on the contrary, was made worse in respect to body than I ever experienced . . . yet I loved Kensington for many reasons". It was to Kensington, not to Chelsea, that he devoted a memento of his "suburban" life—in his *The Old Court Suburb* of 1855.

The seven years during which he saw (less and less of) Leigh Hunt were, on the contrary, only the first stage of Carlyle's attachment to Chelsea. With his "practical steadfastness" he remained there, and in Cheyne Row, for the best part of forty-seven years. For thirty-two years he wrote, lectured, preached and stormed at the Victorian age, suffered in his own peculiar, physical and mental fashion. For the same length of time, Jane Welsh Carlyle, suffered and was kindly, unkindly and brilliant in her fashion. For fifteen years after her death (in 1866), looked after by a niece, his work done and his partner gone, he was still in Cheyne Row, "a gloomily serious, silent and sad old man gazing into the final chasm of things".

In so long and remarkable a tenancy, it was only natural that the people and the house should grow together: that even in the

29 Jane Welsh Carlyle   30 Thomas Carlyle

31 The Carlyle's in their Drawing-room at No. 24 Cheyne Row, about 1858

From a sketch for the painting by Robert Tait

32   Oscar Wilde in 1885

33   A. C. Swinburne
(1837-1909)

gradual accumulation of material objects, it should assume some-thing of their personality and tell of their history in a hundred silent ways. Open to everyone, and now under the auspices of the National Trust, it has inevitably acquired the austerity of a museum, of a place "stripped for action", as it were, the display of "specimens", yet it is heavy with its Victorian memories. An oil painting by R. Tait makes up for some present deficiency of décor by showing us the ground floor dining-room in 1857, the table (on which the visitors' book now rests) covered with an ornamented cloth, the floor, with a flowered carpet, the panelling with a patterned wall-paper. And there, resting no doubt from his struggle (just ending) with his "Minotaur", the *History of Frederick the Great*, is Carlyle himself, in his striped dressing-gown, with the long pipe that, in deference to Jane Welsh, he habitually puffed up the chimney; while she listens, with hand to her lips, in an attitude that may signify attention, reverie—or pain(31).

Victorianism accumulated everywhere; the mahogany chairs with their horsehair seats, the cane and Venetian blinds, the sofa covered with red chintz, where Jane Welsh lay in the tortures of migraine, the steel Bramah grate in the drawing-room, the leather armchair (presented by John Forster) and swivel writing-desk, the elephant letter-weight ... The engravings, of Goethe and Frederick and Cromwell speak of Carlyle's hero-worship. We seem to see him, on the ground floor, eating his "(*dietetic*, altogether simple) bit of dinner"; or with his wife in the evening taking his spoonful of brandy in the first-floor drawing-room. "It was she who widened our poor drawing-room (as if by a stroke of genius) and made it (zealously, at the partial expense of three feet from *her own* bedroom) into what it is now, one of the prettiest little drawing-rooms I ever saw." It was here in the first Chelsea year that he wrote the first volume of the French Revo-lution; and received with the grim stoicism that he had long sub-stituted for "whining sorrow", the news, from the pale and trembling John Stuart Mill, that one of Mill's servants had used the manuscript to light the fire; set to work to rewrite and continue it, with the help of £100 from Mill who added in the fullness of his agonised regret, a set of the *Biographie Universelle*. Here at a later date, famous as reformer—the arch-prophet of many prophets—he entertained his fellow great Victorians, Ruskin, Tennyson, Dickens, Kingsley, Huxley, Owen; his neighbour, the Italian patriot Mazzini, and, on his occasional visits, Ralph Waldo Emerson.

The "sound-proof" room, a converted attic at the top of the house, flimsy and jerry-built as he accused it of being "mere work of Belial, father of lies", remains, a reminder pathetic or humorous as one chooses to look at it, of the crescendo of noise, that subject-ively assailed him in what, for others, was the calm and quiet of Chelsea in the 1850s during his struggle with the history of the Prussian King. The triumph—"all softer sounds were killed and of sharp sounds scarce the thirtieth part could penetrate"—was quickly modified by the fact, the visitor can readily appreciate, that the place was icy in winter and unbearably hot in summer. It is pleasanter to imagine him writing in the garden against the Queen Anne house background that might have been painted by Vermeer. A feeling of discomfort is given to the sound-proof room by the numerous doors, two of which open into the same cupboard. They recall the occasion when an admirer made his way to the top of the house, only to be ignored by Carlyle who sat at his desk, writing. At length, in confusion, murmuring apologies, the visitor backed to the door, and found himself in a cupboard. He tried another with a similar result, embarrass-ment grew frantic. After the third attempt the great man pointed, without looking up. "There, sir, is the door": and went on with his labours.

The interior intensity of life in Cheyne Row was only one aspect of Carlyle's life in Chelsea. As the "sage of Chelsea" he dominated the district. The extraordinary position he came to occupy as the mentor of the Victorian age, not solely as historian or man of letters, but as one with some essential secret of wisdom or recipe of improvement, surrounded even the course of his walks by the river with reverence. The beginning of this special reverence may be traced to the works in which he attacked the social and industrial problems of the "hungry forties". He was "the master", whose *Chartism, Past and Present* and *Latter-Day Pamphlets* inspired the *Hard Times* of Dickens, the *Unto this Last* of Ruskin. Yet as the century advanced, and, after the death of his wife in 1866, he relapsed into rarely broken silence, his long life and continued residence in the one place, as well as his printed works, seemed to foster totemic veneration. The images of which the Victorian artists made so many, the medallion by Woolner in the fifties, the portraits by G. F. Watts and Millais, the portrait by Whistler of 1874, were the icons of the Chelsea print shops; added to the number of visitors who came to waylay the original, and catch a glimpse of the grizzled beard, the clear blue eye, the thin cheek brightly tinged with red, the Inverness cape and wide-brimmed hat of which through the years Mr. and Mrs. Robert Heath made for him so many replicas: which finally seemed inseparable from his main promenade, Cheyne Walk. Not even Sir Thomas More is identified more closely with Chelsea than Carlyle. Woolner's relief on the façade of the present No. 24 Cheyne Row, the bronze statue by Sir Edgar Boehm, erected (1882) in the garden on the Embankment, the year after Carlyle's death, are the fitting local tributes of his era.

In contrast, other Victorian writers are the merest transients. It may be noted that Elizabeth Cleghorn Stevenson, better known as Mrs. Gaskell, was born (1810) in the terrace known as Lindsey Row at No. 93, but has no other connection with Chelsea, her mother dying less than a month afterwards and the child being promptly placed under an aunt's care at Knutsford in Cheshire (the *Cranford* of Mrs. Gaskell's most celebrated book). "George Eliot" at the other extremity of life was there as short a time. George Henry Lewes, the main prop of her existence, was dead two years, she had been married to John Cross for seven months, when early in December, 1880, she and her husband came to No. 4 Cheyne Walk. The great woman novelist was sixty-one and in a melancholy and ailing condition. The move produced the hopeful comment usual on such occasions: "I find myself in a new climate here—the London air and this particular house being so warm compared with Witley."

Yet in less than three weeks (December 22, 1880) she died of a chill caught at one of the St. James's Hall concerts. The arrange-ment of her books "as nearly as possible in the same order as at the Priory"; a few chords on the piano "played with all her accustomed enjoyment", a reading with Mr. Cross of the *Data of Ethics* and the *Study of Sociology* by her old friend Herbert Spencer, a last visit from Spencer himself; such are the slight components of her evanescent association with Chelsea.

At about the same time and for some time after new and exotic currents of thought, opposed to the High Victorian culture, were flowing in the district. They are to be discerned in Tite Street, whence Whistler conducted his campaign against the Victorian artist, critic, and public: where in 1884, Oscar Wilde, just married to Miss Constance Lloyd, came to live, with his bride, at No. 16. Wilde was in his thirtieth year. His youthful displays of audacity and brilliance had already made him well-known as poet, wit and "professor of aesthetics"(32). The *Poems* of 1881 had passed through several editions (though each edition, it is true, consisted of only 200 copies). The comic opera *Patience* in the same year, had established the popular conception of Wilde as a "Bunthorne", a posturing, soulful figure in strange garb. The lecture tours of 1882 and 1883, in America and Britain, had triumphantly preached "the principles of true artistic decoration", the error of antimacassars and waxed peaches under glass. He now appeared (after a visit to Paris) still brilliant but transformed, correctly and fashionably dressed, prepared to cut a figure in Society, together with his "grave, slight, violet-eyed Artemis".

There was more than one reason for settling in Chelsea. His mother, Lady Wilde, the poetess "Speranza", after the death of Sir William Wilde, in 1876, had transferred her salon from Merrion Square in Dublin to Oakley Street. Her house in Oakley Street, Chelsea had become the meeting-place of Irish nationalists, lovers of poetry and disciples of her sons "aesthetic" creed. "All London", said Speranza, "comes to me by way of King's Road . . . Americans come straight from the Atlantic steamers moored at Chelsea Bridge." In Tite Street, moreover, he was not only near the "salon" of which he was the star, but in the same road as Whistler, from whose conversations on art he had already so much profited. An angry and unfriendly Whistler in these days, bankrupt after the libel action against Ruskin, deprived of the White House which he and E. W. Godwin had designed, but installed since 1881 in another studio at No. 13 Tite Street.

The home of the Wildes at No. 16, a plain, red-brick, base-ment house of four floors, with a front bay window passing through three floors, was, as far as the interior was concerned, a challenge to the taste of one who had so much to say about "The House Beautiful". Wilde called in Godwin to help him in the scheme of decoration and that curiously interesting architect (whom Sir Max Beerbohm has described as "the greatest aesthete of them all") added the eclectic flavour char-acteristic of him and something of the restraint on which Whistler had insisted. There was no trace of William Morris's ideas of furnishing, though Wilde in his lectures had frequently quoted him. The peacock feather motif, so frequent in the late-Victorian aesthetic décor, was banned by his superstition: but chairs copied from Greek vase paintings expressed the classical leanings of both Godwin and Wilde and a general simplicity and freshness of colour may be traced to Whistler's influence. The regularity of the continuous frieze of framed etchings that ran round two walls of the drawing-room (after the fashion of Ruskin's Turner water-colours) would not, perhaps, have been disapproved by Whistler himself. The walls and woodwork of the study on the top floor were painted white, in the lower rooms the walls were buttercup yellow, the woodwork lacquered a golden red, the interior doors replaced by curtains. The objects of art included some Whistler studies, and in Wilde's own room, a Monticelli, a Japanese print, a drawing of the triumph of Eros by that favourite artist of the Aesthetic Movement, the decadent Pre-Raphaelite, Simeon Solomon; while a cast of the Praxitelean Hermes stood by the writing-table that had once belonged to Carlyle. There were few of those aesthetic "properties", the fans, the sunflower-patterned screens, with which Du Maurier

surrounded his pictorial parody of Wilde, Mr. Jellaby Postle-
thwaite: yet the many, accustomed to mahogany and horsehair,
thought, or took it for granted, the interior was odd and even
vulgar; incurring the mild rebuke that "Vulgarity is the conduct
of others."

For eleven years, until the thread of his career was broken by
the trial of 1895, Wilde lived at No. 16 Tite Street. The famous
exchange of witticisms and telegrams that followed his criticism
of Whistler's "Ten O'Clock" lecture in 1885, gains in piquancy
from their being close neighbours. It is under the heading
Tenderness in Tite Street that Whistler expresses his sarcastic
acknowledgment to Oscar of "your exquisite article in the
Pall Mall". Wit by telegraph ("when you and I are together we
never talk about anything except me") goes over the electric
wires ("from Whistler Tite Street to Oscar Wilde Chelsea").

There were receptions at Tite Street. During the period when
Wilde was editor of the *Woman's World* and, with Godwin,
interested himself in dress reform, Constance on occasion
received her guests in the "modified form of Greek dress" advo-
cated by her husband and his architectural friend. Brilliant stories,
essays and plays between 1887 and 1893 were written in the top
floor sanctum: yet the association of their author with Chelsea
grew steadily less. The artists of the region (including Whistler)
were not aesthetes. His friendships flourished elsewhere. His
plays—and pleasures—took him into the undomestic and cen-
tralised area of theatres, restaurants and metropolitan meeting-
places; while his wife stayed at home with the two children.
The House Beautiful became the colourless background of a life
lived elsewhere. It is only for a moment or two that Chelsea is
lit by a sinister flash from the bonfire of his career. The Marquis
of Queensberry makes his furious appearance at No. 16 Tite
Street in 1894 and is thrown out. The lurid light briefly illum-
inates the Cadogan Hotel, Sloane Square, in April 1895, where
in the company of Lord Alfred Douglas, the unfortunate man
gulps his hock and seltzer, puffs at cigarette after cigarette, idly
turns over the pages of the *Yellow Book* or gazes dully at the
newspaper reports of the law court proceedings, while he awaits

arrest, a scene of tragedy with a pungently period setting that has
incited Mr. John Betjeman to a poem. In a final sinister gleam,
one sees the disruption of the Oakley Street salon (Lady Wilde
died while her son was in Reading Gaol): the dispersal of the
House Beautiful's contents at a sale that was little better than a
pillage.

It is a contrast to turn to the sojourn in Chelsea of Henry James
—so different in every way from Wilde (whom he is said to have
called a "fatuous cad", and whose *The Importance of Being Earnest*
he is reported, by Hugh Walpole, to have described as "miserable
trash")—tenaciously clinging to respectability and social con-
formity as almost aesthetic ideals. It was towards the end of
Henry James's forty years' residence in England that he came to
Chelsea; in 1911 when he was sixty-eight. Since 1896 his
headquarters had been the delightful Lamb House at Rye.
In 1910 he had made his last visit to America. On his return
he felt the need of town. Lamb House had to be abandoned, at
least for the winter. He could "no longer stand the solitude and
confinement, the immobilisation of that contracted corner in
these shortening and darkening weeks and months". He took
rooms in Cheyne Walk, where he began the fragmentary autobiography contained in *A Small Boy and Others* (1913), *Notes of a
Son and Brother* (1914) and *The Middle Years* (1917). "I apply
myself to my effort every morning at a little *repaire* in the depths of
Chelsea, a couple of little rooms that I have acquired for quiet
and concentration." Presently, his secretary, Miss Bosanquet,
found him permanent quarters at 21 Carlyle Mansions, Cheyne
Walk. In this modern block of flats he felt no nostalgia for old
cream-panelled rooms. The rooms at Carlyle Mansions, looking
over the river were "admirable and ample . . . so still and yet so
animated . . . ideal for work". He found, like Leigh Hunt,
repose in the atmosphere. "I sit here", he wrote to his sister-in-law,
"with my big south window open to the River, open wide and a
sort of healing balm of sunshine flooding the place."

Gouty, dyspeptic, shortsighted (though not incapacitated),
he enjoyed a bath-chair as a luxury: "the long, long, smooth and
really charming and beguiling Thames-side embankment offers

it a quite ideal course for continued publicity, in the sense of variety and tranquillity . . . of jostling against nobody and nothing". His seventieth birthday (April 15, 1913) brought many tributes: a "huge harvest of exquisite, of splendid sheaves of flowers", a "golden bowl" (materialisation of one of his titles) "a very brave and artistic exact reproduction of a piece of old Charles II plate" which sat "with perfect grace and comfort on the middle of my mantelpiece where the rare glass and some other happy accidents of tone most fortunately consort with it".

Then came the war; destroying his conception of the age he lived in but decisively confirming his affection for Britain. The titles of his two, last, projected novels *The Ivory Tower* and *The Sense of the Past*, seemed dissonant in the changed conditions. He chafed to do more than minister to Belgian refugees in Chelsea. "My hands, I must wash them," he said to Logan Pearsall Smith, "My hands are dripping with blood. All the way from Chelsea to Grosvenor Square I have been bayoneting and hurling bombs." There was little he could do except to identify himself with Britain. To be naturalised, would, he jokingly remarked, enable him to say "We" when the Allies advanced. But how did one become naturalised? He asked Ford Madox Hueffer. "You go to a solicitor" the latter suggested. "Good, I will, at once," said James, with fewer words than usual.

It was as a British subject that he died in Chelsea early in 1916, after a stroke. Before the end, Edmund Gosse approached the bed where he lay and whispered "Henry, they've given you the O.M." There was no sign from the apparently unconscious writer: but when Gosse had gone, he said cheerfully enough to the nurse. "Nurse, take away the candle and spare my blushes."

The memorial tablet in the old church identifies him with Chelsea as with the nation and a memorial service was held in the church, where it had always pleased him to remember Sir Thomas More sang in the choir. With the end of a modern epoch and of a remarkable genius it seems appropriate to conclude a brief account of the Writer's Chelsea. It is tempting to wander on into Carlyle Square and pause there in 1916 where, at the performance of *Façade* and with some adaptation of Futurist ritual, an invisible poet, the present Dame Edith Sitwell enounces her poems through drawn curtains and an improved megaphone (called the "Sangerphone"), to the music of William Walton. The influence of Chelsea on the development of Arnold Bennett is an interesting study in itself, yet here it may be enough to remark that Chelsea has not lacked distinguished writers down to the present day.

V

THE ARTIST'S CHELSEA

POPULAR usage terms painters "artists" and though, of course, they are, or should be, so, a somewhat awkward distinction thus tends to be made between them and others who pursue an art, or a craft in which there is a measure of creative and imaginative effort. As far as Chelsea is concerned, painters, numerically, and in their individual importance, are its characteristic artists, but allowance must be made for the others and apology need scarcely be offered for beginning a chapter on "The Artist's Chelsea" with some reference to its eighteenth-century porcelain.

It is true that our history, at its beginning, couples the great name of Holbein with that of Sir Thomas More: we look with interest at his delineation of the More family at home, not only for the persons assembled, but for what indications it gives of the Tudor Chelsea interior—all too slight as they are(3). We speculate on the life of the Dutch flower-painter Van Huysum during his stay in Sir Robert Walpole's household: and in the course of the eighteenth century the record of painting in Chelsea is not entirely blank. Giovanni Battista Cipriani, who was born at Florence in 1727, came to London in 1755 and was a founder member of the Royal Academy in 1768; decorator of the State Coach and author of so many designs skilfully engraved by his fellow-countryman Francesco Bartolozzi; had his connection with the district and was buried in the old churchyard at Chelsea, in 1785, his friend Bartolozzi erecting a tomb to his memory. Paradise Row had its sprinkling of minor painters. The German portraitist John Giles Eccardt, assistant of Vanloo and protégé of Walpole, who painted (1747) the portrait of Thomas Gray, now in the National Portrait Gallery, died in Paradise Row in 1799. Samuel Cotes (1734–1818), miniature painter and brother of the better-known Francis Cotes, lived there: so did John Collet (?1725–80), a disciple of Hogarth, and William

Hamilton, R.A. (1751–1801), one of Boydell's Shakespeare illustrators (and a native of Chelsea). James Northcote, R.A. (1746–1831), whose altarpiece "The Descent from the Cross" is in the present St. Luke's Church, Sydney Street, was staying in "Cheyney Walk" in 1781.

Yet in spite of this muster of worthy but minor painters, the eighteenth-century "artist's quarter", in a more coherent and brilliant sense, was not to be found in Chelsea but in the region of Long Acre, St. Martin's Lane and Leicester Fields. If Chelsea then attained European fame as an "art centre", it was because of its potters rather than its painters. The history of the Chelsea China Factory is not closely documented. Reginald Blunt's exhaustive enquiry into its site led him to conclude, substantially in agreement with Faulkner, that it stood at the upper end of Lawrence Street at the corner of Justice Walk, near "Mr. Tobias Smollett's". In the cellar of the little "Prince of Wales" public-house, Mr. Blunt himself examined "some remains of cylindrical, domed-topped brick structures, which can hardly have been anything but kilns".

It seems to have been established some time before 1745, like the other English factories at Bow and Derby, sought to rival the products of Meissen ("Dresden") and of the French industry. In its early days it produced much uncoloured porcelain, creamy white with a satin glaze, and some Oriental designs in blue and white. In its most flourishing period, towards 1760 (by which time the French factory at Sèvres and the factory at Tournai, in the then Austrian Netherlands, were in full swing), it became "rococo", its products notable for moulded ornament, gilding, and a rich claret colour and "mazarine blue". Success coincided with the management (1749–65) of the Belgian, Nicholas Sprimont, who came from Liège, and had also worked as a silversmith in Soho. It has been suggested that he, and through him the Chelsea factory, had close connections with the Tournai works founded in 1751; an Anglo-Belgian exhibition (1954), at the Anglo-Belgian Institute in London, illustrated the link. There were artist-craftsmen, Duvivier, Willems, Gauron, who worked for both. Mrs. Marsden-Smedley of the Chelsea

Society has pointed out the resemblance in colour and gilding between some Tournai porcelain and that of Chelsea's "gold anchor" period. "Chelsea's *dishevelled bird*", he remarks, "appears as a *oiseau imaginaire* on many a Tournai plate and bowl."

Sprimont, who lived at the nearest house to the old church, in Church Row or Prospect Place as it has also been called (No. 63 Cheyne Walk, largely demolished by bombing in 1941), remained active until 1764. By 1752 the factory was selling porcelain to the value of £3,500 a year, employed a hundred hands and was training a hundred lads, "taken from the parishes and charity schools", in designing and painting. At a somewhat later date, Mr. Boreman, or Bowman, the chief landscape painter, received 5s. 3d. a day, assistants skilled in painting birds, flowers and insects rather less. The paintings included botanical specimens copied from Miller's *Figures of Plants* and an advertise' ment of the time refers to "plates enamelled from Sir Hans Sloan's plants". The Royal patronage, first of George II, then of George III and Queen Charlotte, contributed to the Factory's celebrity. The story, related by Faulkner, after a Mr. A. Stephens, who had it (in 1814) from the foreman of the China Factory (then in the workhouse of St. Luke's, Middlesex), that Dr. Johnson baked his own compositions in the ovens of Lawrence Street, has been often repeated. It is not impossible; and that Johnson by his own unaided efforts should fail to arrive at the right soft-paste mixture is entirely credible; but the story remains an unverified piece of Johnsoniana; its truth scarcely proved by the fact that a set of Chelsea ware came from the Doctor to Mrs. Piozzi.

The first traceable reference to the Johnsonian experiment in Chelsea, appearing in the Monthly Magazine, 1821, under the heading "Stephensiana", is as follows:

> I was told by the foreman of the Chelsea China Manufactory (then in the workhouse of St. Luke's, Middlesex) that Dr. Johnson had conceived a notion that he was capable of improving on the manufacture of china. He even applied to the directors of the Chelsea China Works, and was allowed to *bake* his compositions in their ovens in —— St.,

34   Cheyne Row, built originally about 1708

35 Nos. 90 and 92 Cheyne Walk. Mrs. Gaskell lived in the house next to the one at the end (*left*), Charles Conder in the one on the extreme right

36   Cheyne Walk in 1776

Chelsea. He was accordingly accustomed to go down with his house-keeper, about twice a week, and stayed the whole day, she carrying a basket of provisions along with her. The Doctor, who was not allowed to enter the *mixing* room, had access to every other part of the house, and formed his composition in a particular apartment, without being over-looked by anyone. He had also free access to the oven, and superintended the whole of the process; but completely failed, both as to composition and baking, for his materials always yielded to the intensity of the heat, while those of the company came out of the furnace perfect and complete. The Doctor retired in disgust, but not in despair, for he afterwards gave a dissertation on this very subject in his works; but the overseer, who has read this, assured me in the spring of 1814, that he was still ignorant of the nature of the operation. He seemed to think that the Dr. imagined one single substance was sufficient, while he on the other hand asserts that he always used sixteen, and he must have had some practice, as he has nearly lost his eyesight, by firing batches of china, both at Chelsea and Derby, to which the manufacture was afterwards carried.

The life of the factory in Chelsea was not long. Sprimont, who became proprietor on the death (1758) of Sir Everard Fawkener, the original owner, retired in 1769; William Duesbery took over; the remaining stock and moulds were moved to Derby, when the factory was finally closed and the buildings pulled down in 1784. Yet the china itself—the tureens and dishes moulded in the form of rabbits, doves, partridges, melons and cabbage-leaves; the typical figurines, the scent bottles and trinkets —charming rococo trifles; always retained prestige. Of the four periods distinguished by their marks—"Triangle", "Raised Anchor", "Red Anchor" and "Gold Anchor"—the Red Anchor Period—1754 to 1758—is outstanding in its charm.

To painters the attraction of the river grew with the development of the landscape art itself. It is a tribute to Chelsea Reach that Turner(42), who knew so well the waterways of Britain and Europe; Severn, Humber and Tyne, Rhine and Seine, Tiber and Arno, the Thames in every phase, should, in his old age, choose this particular stretch of river (one imagines him to have chosen the view rather than the house at Cheyne Walk) for daily contemplation. That he liked the view may, of course, be far from the complete explanation of his going to Chelsea (at some

Turner's House

unspecified date in his later years). His secretiveness, his natural tendency to lead two lives, both of which had elements of mystery, led him, no doubt, to "hide" there as an alternative to his main hiding-place in Queen Anne Street. His biographer, Walter Thornbury, makes much of his puzzling absences from his principal address, the perplexity they caused his housekeeper, Hannah Danby, her tracking him to the cottage by the riverside. "The adjoining cottage they [she took a friend with her] found to be devoted to the sale of light refreshments, one of which was the conventional ginger-beer; and the outlay of twopence enabled them to hold a gossip with the proprietor, in the course of which a little judicious interrogation soon satisfied them that the lady and the old gentleman next door must be the great painter and his landlady. They were grieved, however, to learn that the gentleman had been very unwell and that he had seldom been out for the last two months." This, it would seem, was in 1851, for Turner is reported to have died soon after. "On that final day—I believe within an hour of his death—his landlady wheeled his chair to the window, to enable him to look upon the sunshine in which he delighted so much, mantling the river and illuminating the sails of the passing boats."

He had apparently known his landlady at Margate, but perhaps took her name, "Booth", to convey that any name would do to preserve his anonymity. Thornbury discounts the tale of his flourishing a roll of banknotes and declaring he could buy the house—a gesture that does not seem in character, but, garrulous and circumstantial as he was in apocryphal matters, silent on many things it would be useful to know, Thornbury gives no coherent account of the Chelsea period, though it must be admitted his subject did much, in advance, to prevent it. Yet even the atmosphere of mystification causes our fitful glimpses of Turner at Cheyne Walk to be curiously clear. It is evident that locally he stood out as a "character"—the "Puggy Booth" the urchins jeered at, the retired "Admiral Booth" the shopkeepers supposed him to be: through their eyes one can see the short, sturdy figure with that seafaring look he had always had, his face, weatherbeaten by a lifetime so largely spent in the open air, typically that of an old salt. He is plainly in view in the little public-house where he repels the friendly greeting of an artist who recognises him. "I shall often drop in now I've found out where you quarter"—"Will you? I don't think you will," replies Turner, getting up to go. Or on the early morning steamboat to the City, parrying the curiosity of "the gentleman who knew him" and was so surprised to see him there.

As a corrective, however, to Thornbury's, and other highly coloured accounts, one may consider the reference to Turner in Chelsea made by Leopold Martin in his reminiscences of his artist father, John Martin. The two Martins paid a visit to Turner at Queen Anne Street, Cavendish Square, at about the end of 1838. At this comparatively early date (Turner was sixty-three and had thirteen more years of life) it would seem he already had the Cheyne Walk cottage; what is more, did not mind saying so. Martin, it may be added, gives the impression of a clear-headed witness of precise memory.

"Mr. Turner intimated that on my father's arrival he was on the point of walking over to his small place at Chelsea. If inclined for a walk, would he accompany him? This my father willingly agreed to. Crossing Hyde Park, Brompton and so on by the footpaths through market gardens to Chelsea, a very pleasant ramble, Mr. Turner introduced us to a small six-roomed house, on the bank of the Thames at a squalid place past Lindsey Row, near Cremorne House." The respectable Leopold was somewhat offended by its meanness "the house had but three windows in front" and apart from its magnificent view was "miserable in every respect", furnished in the poorest fashion. An old woman (Mrs. Booth, presumably) brought them porter and bread-and-cheese. "Mr. Turner", however, seemed delighted with it all. He "pointed out with seeming pride the splendid view from his single window, saying: 'Here, you see my study; sky and water. Are they not glorious? Here I have my lesson, night and day!'" This is an unexpectedly genial Turner, whose words it may well be give the real secret of the supposedly furtive and eccentric episode—simply, indeed, the quiet study of nature. The roof of the house (Nos. 118-119 Cheyne Walk) was, as one can still appreciate, a good vantage point, from which (wrapped in his dressing-gown) Turner could watch the sun rise and the changing aspects of the river. He is said to have put up the balustrade on the parapet himself and may have bought it second-hand as it is earlier in style than his day. The engraving, in Thornbury's *Life*, of the little bedroom in which Turner died on December 9, 1851 (top hat and umbrella tell, no doubt, of the departed tenant), is spartan enough to justify Leopold Martin's criticism of the furnishing: but for modern eyes, the house itself, as restored by C. R. Ashbee, retains, or has acquired, considerable charm.

Some ten years after the walk from Cavendish Square, John Martin(41), who as the painter of prodigious, romantic effects was at that time freely compared with Turner, settled with his family in Cheyne Walk at Lindsey House. The year was 1848. Turner was still there, in what Ruskin described, in awful capitals, as the House of a Stranger; but Martin, aged sixty, famous for *The Fall of Nineveh* and other stupendous works, probably came to Chelsea because it was cheaper, and considered healthier, than Marylebone where he had previously lived.

The beautiful old mansion was then known as Lindsey Row (Nos. 1-7). Martin occupied the central part (No. 4): which he preferred to call "Lindsey House". It had had distinguished tenants since the days of Count Zinzendorf and the Moravian brotherhood: Joseph Bramah, inventor of the Bramah lock and the modern water-closet; the brilliant engineers, the Brunels, Sir Marc Isambard Brunel, creator of the Thames Tunnel, and his son, Isambard Kingdom Brunel, engineer to the Great Western Railway and designer of the marine colossus, the *Great Eastern*. Martin was the second of several artists to live at No. 4 Lindsey Row, following the Pre-Raphaelite precursor, William Dyce, R.A., who was there 1846–7.

The Victorian arrangement of the house (afterwards No. 98 Cheyne Walk) is carefully detailed by Martin's biographer, Mr. Thomas Balston. The hall had its plaster busts of Queen Victoria, King Leopold, and the painter himself. The front drawing-room on the first floor overlooking the picturesque foreshore, the back drawing-room on the garden, were rich with rosewood furniture. A smaller backroom was Martin's studio. The second floor consisted of bedrooms—a mahogany four-poster in the chief bedroom. Servants slept in the two attic bedrooms above. Martin's library included such appropriate works of reference as Whiston's *Josephus*, Bonomi's *Nineveh and its Palaces* and Abington's *Chaos and Creation*. An impressive piece of furniture was the great carved cabinet of black wood, with its shelves of the medals and jewels he received from European sovereigns, its drawers containing his plans for scientific improve-ments that recall the inventiveness of the Brunels. It was at Lindsey House that Martin embarked on his last huge set of apocalyptic pictures, the "Judgment" series. The Rev. A. Cleve-land Coxe, Rector of Grace Church, Baltimore records a visit there in *Impressions of England, 1851*. "We called on Martin. He was engaged on a picture of the Judgment. Full of his mannerisms and sadly blemished by offences against doctrinal truth but not devoid of merit or interest."

Like Turner, he studied effects of sky, from the balconies on the first and second floors of Lindsey House. He pressed into service the Chelsea boat builder, Charles Greaves, who rowed Turner about the river and whose sheds, rowboats and barges contributed to the picturesqueness of the foreshore. The Greaves family lived near-by at Belle Vue Cottage (No. 91 Cheyne Walk). Charles Greaves' son, the remarkable painter, Walter Greaves, was a child then but lived until 1930, and was able to recall for Sir John Rothenstein (*The Artists of the Nineties*, 1928) how "whenever there was a storm and my father had to stay up all night to look after the boats, Martin used to say to him, 'If there are good clouds and a good moon ring my bell!' When the bell rang, Martin would appear on the balcony to make his sketches"—it is, perhaps, in origin a Chelsea sky that looks on the sensational incidents of *The Great Day of His Wrath* (1853).

The Martins left Lindsey House and the contents were sold after the death of the painter in 1854 (when on a visit to the Isle of Man). The next artist to arrive was Daniel Maclise, who occupied the house from about 1861 to his death in 1870 (he was then seventy-three). His supreme effort on the wall-paintings for the Houses of Parliament, his disappointment at their cold reception (they are still disregarded) are said to have affected the health and spirits of this previously popular and sociable Victorian. He became a recluse, keeping indoors, sitting with his sketchbook at one of the windows looking on the river. He was given, like Carlyle, to complaints about noise, yet his annoyance produced a lively account of the old "free wharf" where, said Maclise, in a letter to *The Times*,

for ever come sailing and oaring in, even in the dead of night, with peculiar cries, as they hoist or lower their masts . . . certain barges called Billy-boys, laden with every kind of material from a brick to a balk of pine 40 feet long. Masses of granite arrive here . . . Three, four or five horses are necessary to pull these importations up an inclined plane from the river and the horses are immersed before my eyes, above their hocks on the coldest of winter days . . . and daily maimed in their goaded endeavours to bring up their load . . .

Meanwhile, the artists' Chelsea, after its earlier nineteenth-century romantic phase (Turner and Martin), had passed into what may be called its Pre-Raphaelite phase with the arrival (severally) of Dante Gabriel Rossetti(38); William Holman Hunt, William Bell Scott and William De Morgan. The house, No. 16 Cheyne Walk, to which Rossetti came in 1862 (aged thirty-four), can be considered, apart from his striking and eventful tenure, as a distinguished building in its own right(24). It belongs to a period for which Pre-Raphaelites, in theory, had no love, having been built, three years after the death of Queen Anne, in 1717, though subsequently it had been much altered. The added bay window to the first and second floors, slender though its supports are, does not spoil the simplicity of the façade with its tall well-proportioned windows. Interior alterations had somewhat disturbed the original simplicity of plan and done away with the main staircase leading to the upper rooms, but though they produced a small labyrinth of corridors, the rooms were still spacious and ample. As well as the large room at the back used by Rossetti as a studio, a drawing-room, forty feet long, runs across the front of the house, and gave him a delightful pre-embankment view of the jetties and beached sailing boats on the shore. The house remains especially distinguished in the beautiful ironwork of railings and gateway. The old description, "Tudor House", was clearly a misnomer, so too, it has been shown, was the later description, "Queen's House". The initials, R.C., on the gate having no reference to "Catherina Regina" (Catherine of Braganza) but to Richard Chapman "of St. Clement Danes, appothecary", for whom the house was built by an unknown but very capable architect in the reign of the first George.

The lover of the Middle Ages in this classic setting might seem out of place, yet the personality of Rossetti took command as decisively as that of Carlyle at Cheyne Row. There was in 1865 that wonderfully Pre-Raphaelite evening party at Cheyne Walk, assembling Edward and Georgiana Burne-Jones, William and Jane Morris, the Ford Madox Browns, Arthur Hughes, William Bell Scott . . . yet many links were snapped or straining. There were later acquaintances present, Swinburne, Whistler and that fascinating "villain of the piece", Charles Augustus Howell. Rossetti's wife was dead and he tried to forget the past in new friends, new diversions and new work. The sitting- and bed-rooms capable of housing three guests, accommodated, off and on, Swinburne, William Michael Rossetti, and Theodore

Watts-Dunton—though not, as originally planned, George Meredith, who speedily decided the ménage was not for him. It was a period when Rossetti began to paint with a professional ease in marked contrast with his earlier efforts; and found a ready market, employing assistants who lived on the premises, W. J. Knewstub from 1863 to 1867, later H. Treffry Dunn. The house by degrees took on the casual, extravagant personality of its tenant.

The garden, then an acre in extent, with an avenue of limes giving on the lawn, witnessed alike his fondness for animals—and mysterious phenomena. A varied procession of birds and quadrupeds, for some of which wire cages were provided, formed the celebrated menagerie: the owls—"Jessie" and "Bobby", rabbits, dormice, hedgehogs, wombats, a woodchuck, a marmot, kangaroos and wallabies, armadillos, a deer, an Irish deerhound, a raccoon, squirrels, peacocks, a jackdaw, a raven, parakeets, chameleons, lizards, salamanders—as well as the zebu (whose eyes, Rossetti said, reminded him of Jane Morris) which cost £20 and proved unmanageable. The shrill cries of the peacocks gave rise to so many complaints that Lord Cadogan thereafter inserted a paragraph in his leases that peacocks were not to be kept.

It was in the garden, too, that the mesmerist Bergheim per-formed, throwing women assistants into a trance, during which one of them picked up a heavy man with no difficulty at all: while in the house, Rossetti and his friends, encouraged by Howell, conducted the spiritualistic séances, at one of which, he tried to call up the spirit of his dead wife.

The spacious and rational conceptions of the early Georgian architect were gradually overlaid by the mystic profusion of objects and ideas. Pre-Raphaelite green crept over the cream-coloured panels, Rossetti's passion for collecting, stimulated both by Howell and Whistler, filled the rooms with a diversity of things. The antique four-poster in his bedroom overlooking the garden was hung with curtains of seventeenth century crewel work: this and other rooms were littered with brass repoussé bowls, old musical instruments, antique chests filled

37 "Dante Gabriel Rossetti in his Back Garden"
From the print after Max Beerbohm

38   D. G. Rossetti, in 1863
From the photograph by "Lewis Carroll"

with jewels, crystals and historic costumes, Japanese screens and fans and specimens of the "Blue and White" Chinese porcelain to which Whistler was especially addicted.

Theodore Watts-Dunton was a constant visitor in the early 1870s. He would put in a morning's work for the *Athenaeum*, sitting at the bay window overlooking the new embankment, before Rossetti came down for his midday breakfast of poached eggs (grumbling at the "baneful and unpoetic habit of early rising"). And Watts-Dunton's bedroom was so sombre in furnishing and crowded with "old carved heads and grinning gargoyles, and Burmese and Chinese Buddhas in soapstone of every degree of placid ugliness" that it acquired the reputation of being haunted. A pencilled note on the fly-leaf of the present writer's copy of *The Life and Letters of Theodore Watts-Dunton* by Hake and Compton-Rickett reads as follows:

"Mrs. Daniel writes: 'No wonder this room of Mr. T. W.'s had the reputation of being haunted for every bit of furniture was black, upholstered with very dark green velvet curtains, the only bit of colour being the famous blue china which was kept in this room.' Mrs. Daniel added 'West Cliff Bungalow was a bright cheerful place after 16 Cheyne Walk. I often went to Mr. John Marshall, D. G. R.'s doctor with notes and messages before taking the journey. Mr. H. C. looked after everything. Miss Lilly H. C. was a very cheerful companion.'"

It seems quite possible that these pencillings were the work of someone directly interested in the compilation of the *Life* (perhaps of Clara Watts-Dunton who added her personal reminiscences) and that the Mrs. Daniel whose words are recorded was the attendant who accompanied Rossetti to Birchington-on-Sea in 1882 shortly before his death, together with Hall Caine (no doubt the "Mr. H. C." of the notes). Hall Caine's sister, presumably, being the "very cheerful companion". Here, in that case, is a fresh fragmentary side-light on the growing sombreness of No. 16 Cheyne Walk in Rossetti's later days.

It is in the early days of his twenty-years' tenancy—when Swinburne(33) was composing *Atalanta in Calydon* in the drawing-room overlooking the river, when he, Howell and Rossetti sallied forth in the evening to taste the pleasures of the town, that we find, apparent, gaiety: in the 1860s, that we visualise the little poet, the bearded painter and their swarthy familiar sampling the *Hermit's Cave*, the *Fairy's Bower* and other raffish attractions of Cremorne.

Then the singular psychological drama that followed the exhumation of Rossetti's poems from his wife's grave, their publication, and the savage attack on the "Fleshly School of Poetry", in the Contemporary Review, in 1871, introduces us to a period of trial—and another Chelsea house, then belonging to Rossetti's friend, William Bell Scott

This was Belle Vue House (No. 92 Cheyne Walk) described by Bell Scott as "a lovely old house close to the Chelsea end of the picturesque old wooden bridge to Battersea, a house built by the Adamses [sic], with a garden buttressed up from the river, and a studio behind to be easily made out of a music-room in which its first owner indulged himself and in which Handel's organ had stood in these former years". Dating back to 1771, with a doorway, masterly in its spacious effect, it may have been the work of Robert Adam, though there appears to be no verification of this. A retired art master, Scott went to live there in 1870 (and remained until the beginning of his last illness—he died in 1890). He tells of the excited appearance of Rossetti at Belle Vue House, wildly shouting "Buchanan", after the appearance of the dreadful article by Robert Buchanan; and of the day in 1872 when William Michael Rossetti (who also lived near by) summoned him to No. 16 Cheyne Walk where "we found our friend [Dante Gabriel] in a condition painful to witness".

Rossetti's various changes of scene in the following period of disorder and malady are no direct concern of this narrative; but we have to take our final (nineteenth-century) look at the house— later renovated by Sir Edwin Lutyens, and today freshly revived in aspect—with Hall Caine in 1880. The façade was smothered in ivy, weeds pushed through the flags of the courtyard; there was worn cocoanut matting on the marble floor in the hall: the cry of the peacock was no longer heard in the silent and neglected garden: the "Blue and White" had vanished from the shuttered rooms: the tenant was a despairing recluse, in two years to end his days at Birchington.

It was Pre-Raphaelitism in more hopeful guise that came to Chelsea in 1872 with William Frend De Morgan, a man then in his thirties, a disciple of William Morris in craftsmanship, friend of Morris and Burne-Jones, determined to revive the craft (and art) of the potter, "within a stone's throw of the old Chelsea China Works". He lived at No. 30 Cheyne Row and rented No. 36, known as Orange House (later replaced by the Roman Catholic Church of the Holy Redeemer) as show-room and workshop, an old coach-house alongside, sheltering a large kiln. With idealism, boyish enthusiasm and the impetuosity of the amateur he there began these efforts that so often (though not always) resulted in delightful tiles. Impatience to complete an order for a thousand tiles "of a fan-shaped flower pattern" caused him to overheat and blow the top off the new kiln. "Many a time", says Miss May Morris, "when our Hammersmith quartette paid a visit to the Chelsea trio, we would go round to Orange House after tea and spend part of the long summer evening wandering through the house and garden eager over the latest experiment." "Experiment" rather than commercial certainty was the word. "There were times when a kiln spoilt cast a slight cloud on the gathering." On the other hand sometimes, from expected ruin would come "a triumph of shining colour": and there were "'spoilt pieces' that one could not help loving for some special quality in them". Yet if a vase, that might, to others, appear satisfactory did not satisfy De Morgan himself he would hurl it to the floor where it smashed in a thousand fragments.

The good work went on in Chelsea until 1882 when De Morgan joined William Morris at Merton Abbey. He conducted his pottery there until in 1887 he married Evelyn Pickering (a Pre-Raphaelite painter in the Burne-Jones manner) and they settled at No. 1 The Vale: a little cul-de-sac, along the King's Road, nearly opposite Paulton's Square and rural in atmosphere. A. M. W. Stirling speaks of the house as a "quaint, rambling dwelling, shrouded in creepers with a veranda back and front . . .

on one side stretched the former deer-park and opposite to it was the lovely spot where Whistler grew his larkspurs and Alfred Austin was inspired to pen 'Farewell summers from a garden that I love'". Inside it was "full of unexpected nooks and irregularities, spruce with gay Morris papers and decorated with De Morgan pots and rich-hued paintings".

The association of the De Morgans with the Vale was a long one, though until 1905 he had his pottery at Sands End, Fulham, before beginning the last remarkable experiment of his old age—the celebrated novels. They were at the Vale in 1909 when the demolition and rebuilding (described in *The Old Man's Youth*) threatened it. The "house-cooling" party, as he termed it with defiant humour, held in that year, recalls the earlier fêtes of Chelsea:

> The guests wandered into an unexpected Fairyland. Old Chelsea Pensioners in their scarlet coats guarded the lane, which was festooned with glowing lanterns. The three houses [those of De Morgan, Professor Oliver and Stirling Lee, the sculptor] and their respective gardens were open to the guests of all . . . in one, a band played softly while nymphs drifted over the turf in picturesque dances . . . in the De Morgans' garden choral singing was interspersed by the song of a living dryad among the bushes, hard by where the head of Pan looked out wickedly from a grove of grass-green lamps . . . in the flower-scented dimness. . . . Then, by-and-by, there was supper and song in the old deer-park beneath the doomed trees wreathed with fairy lamps . . .

It was, said De Morgan himself, "like Cremorne".

Two houses converted into one at No. 127 Church Street were the alternative to the Vale and there De Morgan died in 1917. The tablet to his memory in the old church, designed by Halsey Ricardo, Past Master of the Art Workers' Guild, with wording by Reginald Blunt, was unveiled in the following year.

It was Holman Hunt who unveiled the Rossetti monument in the Embankment Garden (fountain by J. P. Seddon, bust in relief modelled by Madox Brown) in 1887: though long before Rossetti's death their Pre-Raphaelite ways had considerably diverged. Perhaps that occasion recalled to Hunt the youthful period when they had thought of taking the "Queen's House" together: but Rossetti in 1850 had gone to Newman Street: and Hunt to one of the houses, east of Chelsea Church, No. 5 "Prospect Place" (destroyed later to make way for the Children's Hospital). The front room "facing the mid-day sun, was essential for my 'Druid' subject" (*Christians escaping from Persecuting Druids*). On moonlight nights at Chelsea he painted the tendrils of ivy (brought from Surrey) that appear on the door in the *Light of the World* (working from about 9 p.m. to 4 a.m.); attaining a moonlight effect that Carlyle approved when he was induced to pay a visit (doubtful as Carlyle was of "papistical fantasy" in the whole). Between 1850 and 1854 Hunt produced some of his best works at the Chelsea studio, notably *The Hireling Shepherd*. Many years later, in 1879, at another Chelsea studio, this time in Manresa Road, he toiled on the last stages of his *Triumph of the Innocents* and, as he thought, triumphed over the Devil. The Devil it seemed, announced defeat by an explosion that shook the building at the precise moment when Hunt realised he had solved the difficulties of his theme. The diabolic presence (which has less than the usual Pre-Raphaelite definition of outline) may have been the product of the artist's overwrought imagination. Where exactly the studio was in Manresa Road, history does not specify.

The Chelsea of Whistler is less intense, takes on a more realistic air than the various aspects of Pre-Raphaelitism have given it. In spite of his friendly relation with Rossetti at Cheyne Walk, Pre-Raphaelitism was outside his radius: one recalls his sardonic remark on the idealistic craftsmanship of William De Morgan: "Can one forgive a plate for a peculiar shine?" How far it was "Whistler's Chelsea" may, in part, be shown by the fact that between 1863 and 1903, the date of his death, he had some eight different Chelsea addresses.

His first introduction to the district was via the unhistoric region of Victorian expansion, Sloane Street. A young painter, straight from his student experiences in Paris, Whistler stayed in the late 'fifties with his sister and her husband, the surgeon and amateur artist, Francis Seymour Haden, who lived at No. 62 Sloane Street at the corner of Hans Place. Though they shared interest in the graphic process of etching and at this time made some sketching expeditions together, these were outside Chelsea itself. For preference Haden went westwards along the river, in search of the rural distances he drew exquisitely. Whistler on the other hand was attracted to Limehouse and Wapping, producing those superb Thames etchings which remain classics of the copperplate. More relevant to Chelsea are the interiors, which admit us into the placid comfort of an upper middle-class home in Victorian Sloane Street; the etching *Reading by Lamplight* and the painting of the music-room, with Mrs. Haden playing the piano while her daughter, Annie, listens, *Au Piano*, exhibited at the Royal Academy in 1860.

It was natural enough that after a while the young Whistler should wish to live independently; a variety of circumstances took him deeper into Chelsea. He fell out with his respectable brother-in-law, who was offended not only by the Bohemian friends Whistler freely invited over from Paris, but by his association with the *belle Irlandaise* (so much admired by Courbet), the model Joanna Heffernan. He came under the spell of Dante Gabriel Rossetti, and this had its influence probably in bringing him to No. 101 Cheyne Walk in 1863. He stayed there for three years and then in 1866 moved to Lindsey Row (No. 96 Cheyne Walk) with "Jo", and remained there until 1878.

For the best part of ten years, he and his neighbour Rossetti were on most intimate terms. The magnetic personality of the latter exerted its usual effect, No. 16 Cheyne Walk provided a Bohemian circle, a combination of strange characters that Whistler could enjoy, the adventurer Howell with his fantastic stories, Swinburne intoxicated by poetry and life: as well as those beautiful women who came to the house, as models, including the Spartali sisters, Christine and Marie (Marie was to appear in Rossetti's last big picture *Dante's Dream*, Christine was Whistler's *La Princesse du Pays de la Porcelaine*).

There is a point at which Whistler and Rossetti are close as painters and collectors. The handsome, contemplative, self-absorbed feminine type, with traits taken from a whole succession of "stunners", was during this period, the theme of both. It was

Whistler who incited the collecting of Japanese prints and "Blue", though both in different ways became enthusiasts. With Whistler, the enthusiasm was creative in result: it led to that Oriental care for placing and subtle colour harmony that makes his paintings of the river at Chelsea at once so independent of time and place and yet essentially of the district.

The Whistler of the Chelsea "nocturnes" dates from 1866, and after his curious and not entirely explained visit to Valparaiso at the age of thirty-two. The river grew on him in the late 'sixties and early 'seventies. Its subtle evening air was like the blue compounded by Japanese artists for printing their wood-blocks. The old wooden Battersea Bridge was like one of those bridges in which Hiroshige found such decorative possibilities. One imagines the small dandified figure walking in the dusk by the shore, reciting aloud, so as to memorise, a list of the tones, shapes and lights the river presented to his eyes. Sometimes he had himself rowed along the stream by the sons of the boatbuilder Greaves, Walter and Henry. His relation with what he called "the boat-people, a sort of Peggotty family" is another fascinating aspect of the continuance of Chelsea tradition.

The Greaveses knew the ways of painters, of old—Turner and Martin among them. Walter and Henry, captivated by Whistler, themselves turned painters—or were encouraged by him to pursue a natural bent. As boys they had painted heraldic devices on the boats. Walter, who was to become famous, born in Chelsea in 1846, was drawing the river spectacle at the age of fourteen. His famous *Boat Race from Hammersmith Bridge* (Tate Gallery) appears to have been painted about 1862 when he was sixteen. Something more than a masterpiece of "child-art"—a kind of superb "primitive"—it clearly owed nothing to Whistler, though later, both in pictures and in personal appearance, Walter Greaves, who remained Whistler's devoted slave until 1887, did his best to ape "the Master". At the time when the latter broke off relations, Walter was still only thirty-five though he continued to dress like Whistler and imitate, as far as possible, his mannerisms. The time was to come when certain critics hailed him as greater than Whistler (while being his victim), though as Walter Sickert remarked apropos the sensational Greaves exhibition at the Goupil Gallery in 1911: "To be dragged out of your orbit round the town like a tin-kettle at the tail of a dog, by a stronger personality may appear to the un-philosophical an experience merely painful. The truly philo-sophical kettle returns, dented it is true but enriched by, and grateful for, ecstatic experience ... Any nagging about mutual indebtedness is sordid and trivial in such a case. It is as if two lovers should quibble under the bough of a lime tree about which made the other happy." Greaves did not flourish in later years, was eventually admitted as a Poor Brother to the Charterhouse (where he continued to paint Chelsea from memory) and died there in November 1930: but, though overshadowed by Whistler, he made a great personal contribution to Chelsea's pictorial record(1).

Yet in the 'seventies Whistler stood alone. Chelsea's "Japanese artist" brought it triumphantly under the control of his unusual vision—which subordinated even the "Sage of Chelsea" himself to its aesthetic demand. To Carlyle, Whistler was "the creature", incomprehensible (as all painters were); to Whistler, Carlyle was an old man, simply, divested of the Victorian aura, in the famous portrait art proclaimed its triumph over nature. Achieve-ment and comparative success caused Whistler to desire a house of his own. It was at the age of forty-four (and in the year of his libel action against Ruskin—1878) that he moved into the White House in Tite Street, built for him by the architect, Edward William Godwin.

They planned the "ideal house" together, a studio, school for pupils and residence in one; a large studio at the top, (47 feet by 30 feet), a studio drawing-room (30 feet by 20 feet), five bedrooms, dining-room and kitchen; very simple (Godwin proposed a limited application of Greek motives to the mouldings); windows and doors where they were wanted ("and not in Baker Street regularity"); something, indeed (for the time), of an architectural revolution. A light yellow was dominant in the scheme of interior decoration. "To be in Whistler's house," remarked Charles Augustus Howell, "was like standing inside an egg."

39   The Duchess of Mazarin
From the portrait by an unknown artist

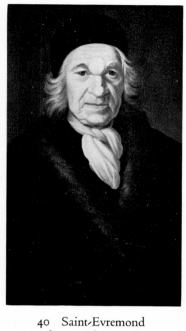

40   Saint-Evremond
From the portrait by James Parmentier

41   John Martin
From the portrait by Henry Warren

42   J. M. W. Turner
From the portrait by Charles Turner

43   Old Battersea Bridge

From the painting by James McNeill Whistler (c. 1865)

His occupancy was a matter of months. He moved in, in October 1878. The trial, with its unfortunate financial result, followed. The bailiffs knocked at the grey-blue door of the new house. Whistler was declared bankrupt in May 1879. The last reception was the scene of Whistler's climbing a ladder to write his witticism over the door. "Except the Lord build the house, they labour in vain that build it. E. W. Godwin, F.S.A. built this one." It was sold, during Whistler's absence in Venice for £2,700 to Harry Quilter, the art critic, whom Whistler never forgave either for his art criticism or for buying and altering the building. The alterations made by Quilter provoked Whistler's protest in the *World*—"history is wiped from the face of Chelsea. Where is Ruskin? And what do Morris and Sir William Drake?"

It was in the 'seventies that Whistler had his closest and most affectionate relations with Chelsea as a subject for paintings and drawings, at the Grosvenor Gallery in 1877 that he exhibited the famous nocturnes the *Blue and Gold—Old Battersea Bridge*, the *Black and Gold—The Falling Rocket*, that so greatly aroused the ire of Ruskin. The latter picture was the original cause of contention and at the court (where this nocturne was brought in upside down) it was argued whether it could really be said to be anywhere. Whistler, of course, disclaimed topography. It was not, queried the Attorney-General cunningly, a view of Cremorne? to which the artist made his reply that "If it were called a view of Cremorne, it would certainly bring about disappointment on the part of the beholders." It was "an artistic arrangement".

Nevertheless, in spite of his disclaimer, he caught the very atmosphere of the river. In a sense he may be said to have created an aspect of Chelsea—which, the eye having once been directed to it, now seems essentially a part of the scene.

A more precise delineation is to be found in the etchings of this decade. Perhaps from one of the Greaves' boats he made his delicate distant view of "Lindsey Row" in 1878: and in 1879 of the old "Adam and Eve" inn. This building (demolished in 1889 in the clean sweep that got rid of a whole row including the tobacco-shop patronised by Carlyle) with its rambling balconies over the water, called forth that feeling for the linear picturesque which Whistler had shown twenty years before in his etchings down-river. The etching of Old Battersea Bridge, also of 1879, is decidedly more descriptive than the painted Nocturne.

In words, Whistler was almost as good about Chelsea as in pictures. The celebrated passage from the *Ten O'Clock* lecture, unwontedly tender, has the mystery and softness of his tone and colour and, unspecific as it is, would merit its place in any Chelsea anthology: "And when the evening mist clothes the riverside with poetry as with a veil, and the poor buildings lose themselves in the dim sky, and the tall chimneys become campanili and the warehouses are palaces in the night and the whole city hangs in the heavens before us—then . . . Nature, who, for once has sung in tune, sings her exquisite song to the artist. . . ."

Chelsea, however, was the headquarters from which, in less tender mood Whistler conducted his fiercely witty campaign against the "priests of the Philistine", the dilettante, the aesthete, and the "intoxicated mob of mediocrity". The development of Whistler's wit would be an interesting study. A certain pointed gaiety was always typical of him. A natural raciness of expression was refined and sharpened by his stay in Paris, his acquaintance with a man of such formidable intelligence as Degas. *L'esprit moqueur* of the Parisian was combined with an American drollery: but the razor's edge was undoubtedly added by Ruskin's attack, the failure of fellow artists to support his case, and the unsatisfactory outcome of his lawsuit. Dispossessed of the White House, he had an understandable bitterness, fomented by the fact that at No. 13 Tite Street, to which he moved in 1881, he was constantly reminded of his loss; and by the delinquency of the White House's new owner, Harry Quilter (the 'Arry of *The Gentle Art of Making Enemies*); as well as the aesthetic pre-tensions of his neighbour, Wilde, at No. 16.

Whistler, as depicted by "Spy" (Leslie Ward—another Chelsea artist who lived in Cheyne Row at Leigh Hunt's old house) in the 1878 *Vanity Fair* cartoon, is a sardonically awesome figure: and this effect was heightened during the 'eighties by his assumption of a quite personal dandyism that was intended to complement and, as it were, illustrate, the wicked polish of his remarks. The monocle screwed in his eye glittered with disdain. A black frock coat was not, in itself, unusual, but Whistler's was longer than fashion decreed, his tall silk hat, taller and distinct in its flatness of brim. His cane was the elegant staff of an eighteenth-century grandee. His white duck trousers, together with the black coat, were deliberately conceived, according to his friend, Mortimer Mempes, as the "harmony in black-and-white which he loved": a calculated relief of colour being provided by the coloured bows in his patent

Whistler. From a sketch by Phil May

leather shoes: or the salmon pink of a prominently displayed silk handkerchief.

In this attire he was as remarkable a Chelsea figure as Carlyle— or Wilde. There is some comedy in the rival dandyisms of Tite Street. Both Wilde and Whistler, in their respective exaggerations of fashion, considered themselves the apex of the *beau monde* and were critical of exaggerations not their own. Thus Wilde's green, frogged overcoat seemed fantastic to Whistler in the flashy reticence of black-and-white, and to require the alliterative rebuke: "restore those things to Nathan's, and never again let me find you masquerading in the streets of my Chelsea in the combined costumes of Kossuth and Mr. Mantalini".

The wordy warfare with Wilde reached its height in the exchanges that followed Whistler's exposition of "Art for Art's Sake" in the *Ten O'Clock* lecture delivered at the Prince's Hall (February 1885); though Whistler's bolts were now hurled from a new address. He rented a studio, No. 454 Fulham Road, in 1885, in the following year was installed at No. 2 The Vale, with Maud Franklin who had replaced the red-haired beauty, Joanna Heffernan, as "Mrs. Whistler". It was, like the house of William De Morgan opposite, a comfortable, verandaed early-nineteenth century piece of domestic architecture, semi-detached but with a large garden. Straitened circumstances or good taste, or the two combined, gave the interior, with its sparse furniture, yellow-washed walls and matting on the floor, an almost Japanese simplicity. Here, if the words of William De Morgan's biographer are to be taken literally, Whistler "cultivated his larkspurs" (an unexpected condescension to nature). It was in this house, at a later date, that Charles Ricketts and Charles Shannon, established the Vale Press, which has its place in the history of fine book production and has helped to preserve the memory of the now demolished little rural cluster of four houses.

Oscar Wilde, a great friend of Ricketts and Shannon, took William Rothenstein with him to see them at the Vale in the 'nineties. The place was still simple and fresh in colour, with its primrose walls and apple-green shelves, though the pictures on the wall (besides Shannon's lithographs)—a fan-shaped water-colour by Whistler, a drawing by Hokusai—already hinted at the treasures these fastidious collectors would later amass. As Rothenstein describes them they seem a strangely Pre-Raphaelite couple (they were, indeed, in that tradition), bent over their blocks for wood-cutting "like figures from a missal". Oscar Wilde, a regular visitor, compared the pale, ascetic Ricketts with his red-gold beard to an orchid, Shannon, fair and fresh-complexioned, to a marigold; while their taste, conversation and the idealism of their own work, attracted a circle in which the craftsman, like Sturge-Moore and the connoisseur, like the young Roger Fry, both joined.

Whistler, to go back a little, remained at No. 4 The Vale for four years. While he was there he married the widow of his architect friend, E. W. Godwin (who died in 1886). In 1890 they moved to No. 21 Cheyne Walk. Two years after, Whistler's exhibition at the Goupil Gallery proved a great success, the tide of opinion had turned in his favour, as a painter of European fame, he decided to leave London for Paris.

In theory, at least, Whistler attached little importance to a place (or a country) of residence. The artist in his sublime independence could live anywhere. If he chose Paris to live in, it was for the understanding company of confrères, a climate of opinion more congenial than he had found in London. In anticipation of the respect he would enjoy as a Master, he was able to uproot himself without pain from the Chelsea to which he had given the personal and possessive adjective "my".

Yet Chelsea was his one refuge in emergency, his point of rest. In the rue du Bac in Paris he kept open house and revived those hospitable breakfasts that had been an institution of the Tite Street days: but painting in Paris was moving into a new phase, unsympathetic to his delicate art. The writers—Mallarmé and Huysmans among them—paid him tribute, but the younger painters showed no wish to sit at the feet of "the Master".

He returned to England when his wife fell ill; her death in London, in 1896 made him homeless indeed. In the last seven years of his life, he stayed, fitfully, in several places but returned at last to Chelsea. It was at No. 74 Cheyne Walk, a house built by C. R. Ashbee on the site of a fishmonger's shop (of which Whistler had made a lithograph), that he died in July, 1903 at the age of sixty-nine. Once again the memorial service of an illustrious man was held in the old church, attended by a few artists and people who had known him (among them Joanna Heffernan, the *White Girl*, now an old woman): though the grave of Whistler, with that of his wife, is at Chiswick. The two contemporaries in Britain whom Whistler most admired were Albert Moore and Charles Keene. Topographically, Moore belongs to Kensington—a fact which recalls how far the classic (and academic) school of the late Victorian age was centred in the Royal Borough, Chelsea never possessed so imposing a constellation of studios as that of Melbury Road and Holland Park Road, where the representatives of what Ruskin termed a "senatorial and authoritative art" reigned in grandeur. This may be fortuitous. It would be stretching generalisation too much to say that Kensington was "classic" while Chelsea was "realist" or "impressionist". The gentle and unsenatorial Moore might as well have lived in the King's Road as in Holland Lane —though it is less easy to imagine Lord Leighton than Whistler in Chelsea haunts. It excites no surprise, however, that Keene should have lived in Chelsea. He moved in 1873 (while Whistler was at No. 96 Cheyne Walk) from rooms over Elliott and Fry's in Baker Street to "Paradise Row" (No. 11 Queen's Road West). He rented rooms there from F. Wilfrid Lawson, one of two painter brothers, the other, Cecil Gordon Lawson (d. 1882), who painted several pictures of Cheyne Walk and neighbourhood, being considered, in his own time, of unusual promise.

Here the bachelor Keene, aged fifty at the time of the move and famous as *Punch* artist, made his beautiful drawings amid a jumble of illustrator's "properties"—old swords, iron gauntlets, the torso of a wooden horse with saddle, old female costumes, rustic smocks and waistcoats, musical instruments, bagpipes, and folios of prints collected through many years. In the small kitchen, if not dining out, he would concoct his own evening meal, a stew of beefsteak, potatoes and onions, left to simmer on a gas jet, and this he would eat at five o'clock, reading a book the while and invariably concluding the meal with bread and jam. This mildly Bohemian routine continued at No. 239 King's Road, to which Keene moved in 1879—the apparatus by which he cooked his meals here appears to have comprised a jam pot and the spring from a "gibus" hat over a gas burner brought by a long tube to a stool in the middle of the room. He smoked the hideously pungent mixture provided by the caked dottles of many past pipes and lamented that in these respectable quarters, where there were other tenants, he was not permitted to make that melancholy drone on the bagpipe which was his favourite recreation.

A tall man, with straggling pointed beard, habitually dressed in loosely cut tweeds and wearing a "billycock" hat, he added to Chelsea's curious medley of fashion in the 'eighties, though in appearance he was, more than others, the "typical artist" as the layman has come to imagine him. His life in the King's Road (where he stayed until 1839, three years before his death) seems very self-contained, though he had his acquaintances in the district as well as his quietly satisfactory friendships elsewhere.

We should not expect to see him at breakfast with Whistler and his disciples in Tite Street—though it is pleasant to remember that they knew and respected each other's art with equal admiration. On the other hand, while a *Punch* draughtsman had little in common with what Keene called "the Pre-Raphaelite set", he was friendly with Bell Scott, whose collection of first editions he admired at Belle Vue House: where he astonished Bell Scott by revealing an unexpected intimacy with "Fitzgerald, the old scholar at Woodbridge, Suffolk".

A letter in which Keene records this Chelsea conversation is interesting not only in its attempt to imitate, or caricature, the "Pre-Raphaelite" manner of speech but also in its awareness of the gifts of the "old scholar at Woodbridge". It is not likely that the translator, or creator, of Omar Khayyam, saw a great artist in Keene; it is certain the latter could not believe Fitzgerald capable of a poetic masterpiece: but on Keene's casual mention of their acquaintance (1881) Bell Scott "jumped off his chair! 'Do you know him? Why Ram Jam' (some wonderful Persian name he gave it) 'is the most quite too exquisite work of the age and Rossetti considers the translations from Calderon the finest thing . . .' etc. etc. So [continues Keene] I shall tell the old man. I don't know whether he'll be pleased."

It is a commentary on the overlap of artist generations that Keene, who was a star of *Punch* in 1860 should have known Walter Sickert (who lived until 1942), put him up for the Arts Club and at the time of his last illness gave Sickert a choice of what drawings of his he liked to have. Keene, indeed, seems nearer to the "Impressionism" of the end of the century than Whistler himself. When he died, Chelsea was already in a post-Whistlerian phase, with the "impressionists" of the New English Art Club, who included Sickert; although, in more general terms, the combined magnetisms of its great men had really, at last, constituted it an "artist's quarter", irrespective of any particular faction. Even so cosmopolitan an artist as Charles Condor settled there at last, living at Belle Vue Lodge from 1901 to his death in 1909. When the young William Rothenstein arrived in London from studentship in Paris, Whistler observed, "Of course you will settle in Chelsea," as if an artist could settle nowhere else.

That Sickert "settled" there, would be too much to say, in view of his lifelong restlessness and also of that love for the shabbier districts of London that associates him with Camden Town and Kentish Town, Clerkenwell and Islington. It is not easy to follow his movements with precision from the 'eighties when he gave up acting and became a "Follower", helping Whistler prepare his etching plates in Tite Street. He went to France, met Degas, lived at Dieppe, married and took a house in Hampstead painted the music-halls of North London; all before he paused in the Vale in 1893, and for a time, rented No. 1 from the De Morgans and received pupils in a "school", as the prospectus asserted, "under the patronage of Whistler"; the pupils at evening classes including William Rothenstein, Roger Fry, and that historian of the New English Art Club, Alfred Thornton. Sickert, according to Thornton "loved the red-faced sporting men with big-buttoned, box-cloth coats, who thronged the King's Road, and the racy retorts of the dingy little London *gamine* as she strolled the streets of Chelsea". According to Rothenstein, he had a place of work, other than Mrs. De Morgan's studio "a small room at the end—the shabby end—of the Chelsea Embankment, west of Beaufort Street. Needless to say, this room was in one of the few ugly houses to be found along Cheyne Walk." Sickert's interest in plebeian life and décor was a puzzle to his contemporaries. He is said, when passing a rag and bone shop with Steer, to have remarked, "That's how I should like my pictures to look." Steer, a man of few words which sometimes achieved the effect of wit by accident, said, "They do."

Otherwise, he appears simply as a visiting confrère among those who assembled socially round Philip Wilson Steer, the leading light of the New English Art Club and most firmly and indisputably settled in Chelsea from 1898, when, at the age of thirty-eight, he took No. 109 Cheyne Walk—where he remained for forty-four years. It was one of the late-eighteenth-century houses, given, externally, a Victorian appearance by altered windows. Steer had a studio built at the top but did not use it for long. The spacious first floor with its three tall windows overlooking the river provided both a sitting⁄ and painting⁄room. Here, in placid bachelor state, he entertained his friends, would doze in peace while George Moore talked endlessly of Manet, or Henry Tonks, the martinet of the Slade School and D. S. MacColl, critic, watercolourist and "the Ruskin of the Impres⁄ sionists", argued about regrettable modern tendencies in painting.

There had always been collectors in Chelsea, and in this respect Steer followed in the steps of a More, a Sloane a Rossetti. By degrees he filled the house with the finds of the sale⁄room and the little antique and lumber shops of the King's Road: Chelsea china, coins and medals, Oriental screens, paintings and bronzes. Sickert's portrait of Steer as a young man, a nocturne by Walter Greaves, water⁄colours by Sargent, Tonks and other friends hung on the walls. The cosiness of the interior is reflected in one of Henry Tonks's humorous conversation pieces, where the light gleams on the Chelsea figures behind the scrupulously polished glass of the cabinet and Steer, a bulky foreground presence, pours out tea for his old nurse and housekeeper, Mrs. Raynes, and a party of her friends. Mrs. Raynes, whose portrait by Steer hangs in the Tate Gallery and who lived to be ninety (she died in 1925), must be numbered among Chelsea characters, if only for her excellent remark, when complimented on a pudding—"There's art in everythink, even in painting pictures." Steer was greatly attached to her and hardly less to his tabby cat, "Mr. Thomas", who lived to the ripe feline age of eighteen.

The years passed quietly. Every winter, Steer laid his plans and took infinite precautions against the enemy that annually invaded the snug house on Cheyne Walk—the common cold. Regularly as clockwork, he packed up in the summer and went off for his sketching outing, often accompanied by his close friend, Ronald Gray (a painter, Chelsea born, whose father had an engineering business in Danvers Street). Steer loved shopping and, with his string bag and his dog "Peter", was a familiar figure at the fruit and vegetable stores of World's End.

Few events rippled the gentle surface of Chelsea existence. "Flo", a girl from Fulham, took Mrs. Raynes's place as housekeeper and served "Father", as she called Steer, until the end. The great "Mr. Thomas", the cat, died of influenza in 1924 and was replaced by a "powerful striped tabby", who stalked seagulls on the mud banks of the shore. The Thames flood of 1928 that swept into Chelsea and Millbank (destroying many works in the basement of the Tate Gallery) invaded the basement of No. 109 Cheyne Walk, the dog being rescued from water six feet deep. Steer was still living in Chelsea when war began in 1939 and stayed there until the year of his death, 1942. The fabled labyrinth of underground Chelsea provided an air-raid shelter, the main wall of the basement being discovered, as Steer's niece, Miss Hamilton, has recorded, "to be of great strength and age, being part of one that had run down to the River since Tudor times". Old and nearly blind, he endured patiently the discomforts of the period. His back windows were blown in, and the roof of the house damaged by bombs, though a greater source of grief towards the end was the destruction of the old church. Steer's house was again damaged by rockets after its owner's death.

So long a life is both near to and far from our own day. More distant in every way is John Singer Sargent, yet for many years he and Steer were Chelsea neighbours and great friends. Sargent, the young cosmopolite, an American born in Florence, arrived in London from Paris in 1885, taking a studio at No. 13 Tite Street in succession to Whistler and, in the following year, joining in the "Impressionist" venture of the New English Art Club, with Steer, Charles Furse and lively spirits of the time. He took a twenty-one years' lease of these premises in 1900, though he also had a large studio, Nos. 12–14, The Avenue, Fulham Road, where he worked on his decorations for the Boston Library and Museum (it was here that he painted the generals of the 1914 war and the war picture *Gassed*).

It was during the 'nineties that he began to paint the portraits which made him so much sought after. Sir Max Beerbohm has depicted the fashionable queue outside No. 31 Tite Street, the burly painter peering from the window at the row of distinguished would-be sitters, including Lady Faudel Phillips and the Duchess of Sutherland, a number of messenger-boys keeping the place of others. The Hon. Evan Charteris has related in his Life of Sargent that on one occasion a "famous personage" asked to bring some of her friends to a sitting. He having doubtfully agreed, a crowd of "curiously dressed representatives of the aesthetic movement" arrived, the pressure of arrivals forced the painter into a corner, aud the sitting had to be abandoned.

His real home in Chelsea was the flat of his sister, Emily, in Carlyle Mansions, where he dined with her, another sister, Mrs. Ormond, and their mother in a room hung with red damask overlooking the Thames, or they jointly entertained friends, Steer, Tonks, Henry James, and some of the American painters who in the early years of the century had not yet abandoned London for Paris. On these occasions, Sargent, who was tongue-tied on public occasions, would talk freely, expressing definite views on art, in which he was curiously bigoted (seeing that his appreciation of music and literature was quite wide). In some ways, and certainly in antipathy to public speaking, he and Steer were alike. They differed, obviously, on the score of travel.

Unlike the stay-at-home Englishman, Sargent found Chelsea, and the English climate, possible for only four months of the year. Within this period, his current portrait commissions had to be completed: the months remaining were spent in Venice, Rome, or elsewhere in Europe. His bags were always packed ready for instant departure, his transatlantic crossings were a record in number: and to this extent Chelsea was less a part of his being than it was of Steer's. It was in Chelsea, however, though on the eve of a visit to the United States, that he died in 1925. He had gone home after a farewell dinner at No. 10 Carlyle Mansion (Steer and Tonks, as so often, among the guests), the next morning the maid at Tite Street found him dead— an open volume of Voltaire's *Dictionnaire Philosophique* by his side.

His Chelsea studios were full of paintings, studies and the

water-colour landscapes which were his recreation. Steer, who helped to arrange a public sale was astonished when the first day brought £146,000.

In outward appearance, and as a whole, Tite Street (named after the architect Sir William Tite) is far from being one of the most attractive thoroughfares of Chelsea. It does, however, represent interestingly that late-nineteenth-century phenomenon, the studio-house. There can have been few, if any, specially designed, top-lit studios in London before the 'sixties: though the unmoneyed painter would find an incidental advantage in the skylight of his attic. Others painted happily, as the old masters did, in the spacious rooms of old houses, not being over-particular as to the direction in which the tall side-windows faced. This was the practice of Wilson Steer at No. 109 Cheyne Walk. He did not care to use the studio he added and was not averse from the entry of the sun into his painting-cum-drawing-room.

Yet, the professional studio, properly so-called, with a large top, or top-and-side north light, was considered desirable on various counts. It reflected, from the 'seventies to the early years of this century, a growing opulence and the uniqueness of the artist's professionalism. It reflected an attitude, that set importance on the faithful reproduction of a given object under a steady and unchanging (north) light. For both reasons it had its value for a portrait painter like Sargent. He received his sitters in appropri-ately magnificent surroundings, and was able to study them with-out the distraction of shifting shadows and fugitive gleams. These considerations applied generally; but the studios of Tite Street also reflect the tendency of Chelsea to become a com-munity of painters and sculptors: and something of a community feeling caused the same architect to be employed on the design of their homes and workshops—E. W. Godwin.

The White House designed for, and in conjunction with, Whistler, by Godwin, encouraged others to commission him. The young Archibald Stuart-Wortley, who bought three plots of ground adjoining the White House, required a larger house to be built on this site. George Francis (Frank) Miles, a devotee of Japanese art and portraitist in pencil, was another client, for whom Godwin devised a house of nine rooms with a studio at the top, forty feet long. It was not an easy specialisation. "The artist", said Godwin, "is the most extraordinary client that you can deal with—every individual painter has his individual idea as to what a studio should be. One tells me that he wants the light to come straight down from the roof. Another says he must only have a window light. While Pellegrini ['Ape' of *Vanity Fair*] declares he will have nothing but light—walls and roofs, all must give light. One would be driven mad if he had many artists as clients." On the other hand, difficult too was the Board of Works, where the plan submitted for Miles's house was considered "worse than Whistler's", and would only pass with the addition of what Godwin described as "a number of remi-niscences of a visit to Holland".

In all, Godwin was responsible for, as at present numbered, No. 35 (the White House of 1879), No. 33 (The Studios), No. 29, and opposite, No. 44 and the neighbouring Tower House. No. 31, where Sargent died, was the work of another architect, R. W. Edis. In view of this and the varying require-ments of client and authority, it is hardly surprising if the group is not altogether coherent as an architectural composition, though that it is a group is apparent enough.

Tite Street and Cheyne Walk were not by any means the whole of the artist's Chelsea in the late nineteenth century. The penurious painter or sculptor could get a workshop converted or easily convertible into a studio, at a very small rent. Thus, the Avenue Studios in the Fulham Road, where Boehm, Alfred Gilbert and Poynter worked were previously the work-shops used when the Onslow Gardens estate was built. In Manresa Road, the site of the Public Library and L.C.C. Technical School was occupied by a row of ramshackle buildings used as studios, facing the Trafalgar and Wentworth Studios on the other side of the road (where Wilson Steer, Sir Frank Brangwyn and Sir Frank Short among others worked in their early days). The specially built studios in Glebe Place, completed about 1890, were, the late Ronald Gray records (in some interesting unpublished notes on the origin of the

Chelsea Arts Club), considered "very smart". Gray then had "one of the glass shacks in Glebe Place opposite Bramerton Street".

That famous institution the Chelsea Arts Club came into being very naturally and spontaneously in this studio world. Chelsea was still somewhat cut off from the metropolis, the local deficiency in congenial places of resort and refreshment was all the more obvious. Two small Italian café-restaurants served the growing artist population, one, Manzoni's, almost opposite Carlyle Square, the other, the Monaco in the King's Road, which later became the "King's Head". Some would go for food and drink to the "William IV" in the Fulham Road, or to the "Six Bells" which was then pretty much like a country inn: but socially there was still something lacking. Artists began to meet as a group, for beer, bread-and-cheese and talk, in the studio of one or other. It was a logical step as well as a greater convenience to form a club: in 1891 the Chelsea Arts Club was launched at No. 181 King's Road, premises belonging to a Scottish painter, James Christie.

Whistler was one of ninety artists who expressed their willingness to join. The story is told of a foreign painter with a pronounced accent, who proposed that meetings should be held at the Pier Hotel. "Oh, no! not a *beer* hotel," said Whistler, affecting to misunderstand the pronunciation of the labial. There was some fear that Whistler's fame would require his election as president of the club. The memory of his stormy presidency of the Royal Society of British Artists, when, as he said, "the artists went out and the British remained", was still fresh. It seemed a happy solution to have no such permanent office. A sculptor, Thomas Stirling Lee, acted as the first chairman. He is described in A. S. Hartrick's reminiscences as "the most innocent and inoffensive of men" who became notorious because of a nude in a panel for St. George's Hall, Liverpool, which aroused an acute fit of morality. With Lee as chairman and Whistler safely relegated to a committee of rules, the Chelsea Arts Club started off smoothly and quickly acquired the distinct and genial individuality it still retains.

This distinct character was due in part to the fact that only practitioners in some branch of visual art were eligible as members—a rule in which it is unique among London clubs: to the fact also that it was purely social and not concerned with exhibiting works of art. An early proposal for annual exhibitions was quickly shelved: nor did it propagate any particular theory, though Whistler's brilliant exposition of "Art for Art's Sake", the *Ten O'Clock* lecture, was re-read at the club on a memorable evening in 1891.

In 1902 the club moved to the premises it still occupies at No. 143 Old Church Street, a pleasant building with its low, asymmetrical façade, its informal and varied garden front; the garden itself, with its trees and flowers and cupid fountain, by Henry Poole, R.A., as delightful as any of those for which Chelsea is famous.

The history of such an institution is better conveyed by personalities than dates. Retrospectively one sees Whistler arriving in his hansom to deliver some carefully prepared *bon mot*; or at the dinner given in his honour when he spoke of being misunderstood, likening himself to the Traveller in the old tale who drew his cloak more closely about him when the stormy winds blew, to cast it open when the sun shone again—the sun being the genial atmosphere of the Chelsea artists in their club. Or Sargent in the agonies of after-dinner speaking, scoring the table with deep scratches from a fork clutched in nervous hand; or his equally inarticulate friend, Wilson Steer, bent over the chessboard. . . .

With its resources of talent and gaiety, the club inspired that unique festival the Chelsea Arts Ball. Its origin has been traced to the fancy-dress dances and Mardi Gras parties organised by the members, among whom the sculptor Stirling Lee was particularly active in the attempt to create a Parisian verve. The parties became progressively more ambitious: and according to the reminiscences of Ronald Gray, one of them, held at the Chelsea Town Hall, was the direct precursor of the Chelsea Arts Ball, which except for the war years has been held annually since 1908, and, at the Albert Hall, is a more brilliant and tumultuous Ranelagh in a still larger Rotunda. The décors designed by members of the Chelsea Arts Club form an interesting episode in British theatrical design, though strictly speaking the history of the Ball takes us outside the limits of Chelsea itself—it may be looked on as Chelsea's gift to London.

James Pilton's Menagerie in King's Road

VI

IMAGES OF CHELSEA

HAVING surveyed the history of painters and other artists in Chelsea one asks what record of it they have left: and even whom one might elect as best conveying the spirit and character of the region. The obvious answer to the latter question is Whistler. Has he not given us that dimly exquisite and poetical Battersea Bridge? distilled the subtle magic of riverside atmosphere and echoed distant festival in the slow golden descent of the rockets of Cremorne? All this is true, yet of course we should not call Whistler a topographer, nor say that his images are, on the whole, local. There is the same atmospheric poetry in his picture of Valparaiso Bay. In his cultivation of art for its own sake, for the sake, that is, of some beauty of form or colour, he escapes from particular association. His Battersea Bridge of the nocturne is an element in a generalised design (though he painted a more detailed view(43)). Similarly, his Thomas Carlyle is scarcely to be studied as a character portrait of the Sage of Chelsea, the "man in his time"; it has more to tell us of Whistler's flawless sense of arrangement.

Topography, in which there is fact and description is more pedestrian though, in the present context, that is, to tell us what Chelsea has looked like, it has a more definite use. Kip's famous view of Beaufort House(6), 1699, admirable specimen of the engraver's craft and not without its aesthetic attraction of design, is primarily of value for the information it gives. The "arrangement" here is not that of the artist's invention but objectively of Chelsea at the end of the seventeenth century. In the right foreground we see "Duke Street" and the beginning of Lombard Street, and the ferry boat starting on its way across. Behind Duke Street is the trimly laid out orchard and the terrace of Beaufort House, the quay of which appears to the left. The eye travels from the landing-stage, along the Front Court of Beaufort House, past the lodges with their pointed roofs, to the Inner

Green Court and so to the great house itself, the formal gardens behind it and, in the distance, the King's Private Road. In the left foreground is Lindsey House, behind it Gorges House and garden, and then the stables of Beaufort House. To the right of the engraving is the garden (with circular lay-out) of Danvers House, behind it, Dovecote Close, the kitchen-garden of Beaufort House. As a document, this engraving is indispensable for the historical study of Chelsea.

That topography, the representation of architecture and art of a high order are not incompatible, there is Canaletto to remind us. His painting of the interior of the Ranelagh Rotunda (National Gallery)(19), executed, as the inscription in his own handwriting on the back of the canvas records, in London, 1754, is both delightful to look at and of value in the confidence it gives us that we have now seen exactly what Ranelagh was like. It was towards the end of Canaletto's several years stay in England, when a certain mechanical dexterity was becoming noticeable in his style; yet the groups of figures here are natural-looking, and the Venetian master's skill deals superbly with the chandeliers, the ornament and intricate perspective imparting an Italian stateliness to the setting which is lacking in the popular prints of Ranelagh by Bowles of about the same time.

The early English water-colourists were to some extent in the Canaletto tradition (did not Girtin learn much from the Canaletto drawings in Dr. Monro's collection?) and their own combination of architecture, social life and landscape has included views of Chelsea that interest us from each of these points of view. The obscure James Miller, who exhibited views of London and its environs at the Royal Academy and the Incorporated Society of Artists from 1773 to 1791 made a charming picture of Cheyne Walk in 1776(36), a little west of the end of Oakley Street, showing the sign of the old Magpye Inn hanging on a beam over the road, and the inn's convivial box built over the shore, one of several in the days before the Embankment. It is delight-fully intimate and the play of shadow from the tree on the brick-work (which is, convincingly, Cheyne Walk brick) is a typical effect still to be appreciated in photographs of modern Chelsea.

There is a sensation of cheerful noise (such, however, as would have maddened Carlyle) of gossip along the fenced walk, the clack of hooves, the shout of a carter or riverside character who somewhat dwarfs his surroundings by his over-heroic proportions, the rumbling of barrels, trundled along a gangway to a barge. In the distance appears the White Windmill of Battersea.

A later water-colour of Cheyne Walk (1811) shows that unequal and prolific painter John Varley at his best. The church, which still has the original cupola that was removed four years after the date of Varley's water-colour, is tenderly silhouetted, the piers of Battersea Bridge make an enticing and delicate pattern in the intervals between the dark foreground trees, composed with all Varley's art-master science, but less than usually conventional. The wooden awning of the shop on the right survived into Victorian times(45).

The spirit is the same, though bonnet, shawl and crinoline tell of the new age in the lithograph (c. 1850), looking along Cheyne Walk, by Church Row, or Prospect Place, from the old church (with Sir Hans Sloane's tomb on our right)(44). The trees and wooden rail along the river are as they were, but since Varley's time the houses have evidently been somewhat remodelled, early-Victorian balconies add their gaiety; the first house visible behind the church is No. 63 Cheyne Walk (shattered in the twentieth century by bombs) and taking the numbers consecutively one can just see at the corner No. 59 and the window of the first floor in which, even at the time of this lithograph, Holman Hunt is painting, or at all events is very soon to paint, *The Light of the World*. The conspicuously new item in the scene is the portentous gateway (suspension bridge in embryo) of the Cadogan Pier. Its air of modern improvement, not unpleasantly combined with quasi-rustic leisure, is seen to closer advantage in the minor Victorian painter Brownlow's open-air genre-piece(46), where the eye strays from the goat-carriage in the foreground to the admirably realised shirt-sleeved lounger, apple-woman, plodding Chelsea pensioner, and brisk top-hatted man of business making no doubt for the steamboat to the city.

To revert to our water-colours, art and fact mingle in Thomas

Rowlandson's drawing of the finish of the race for Doggett's Coat and Badge at the Old Swan Inn, though Rowlandson, always interested in any sporting event, concentrates attention on the action of the watermen and the cheering crowd, on the shore and in the line of barges drawn up for the finish and treats a little summarily, although with spirited "calligraphy", the "Swan" itself, while church and farther distance seem hazily remem/ bered(16). It is, however, a triumph of graphic vigour. Girtin's *White House* must be numbered among the masterpieces that Chelsea has inspired, though, like Whistler's nocturnes, of which it may be considered an anticipation, it transcends topography.

It is sad that no masterpiece by Turner has come down to us depicting the Chelsea he studied so attentively—perhaps surprising also. It would seem that in those later days, the sky and river he saw from his Cheyne Walk eyrie became an inner or imagina/ tive vision, that the sun was converted into the sun of Venice, that he looked beyond the Thames to stranger and wilder waters. While it is certain he found Chelsea inspiring it is equally certain he did not make it his theme.

For our early nineteenth/century picture of Chelsea in water/ colour, apart from such rare examples by practised hands as Varley's Cheyne Walk and Bonington's view from the Red House, Battersea, we descend to the worthy though amateur level of the Gulston Collection in the Chelsea Public Library which provides fifty views of buildings, unique in many cases as record but marked by a primitive simplicity of execution. They were painted by, or for, Miss Eliza Gulston, Faulkner's assistant in the preparation of his History of Chelsea. "From local sources we learn", says Reginald Blunt, in his introduction to the catalogue of *Chelsea a Hundred Years Ago*—an exhibi/ tion held at the Town Hall in 1929, "that Miss Eliza Gulston lived at Ashburnham Cottage, which stood near the river just west of Ashburnham House, at the western end of Chelsea. . . . The water/colour drawings in this collection may have been her work, but it seems more probable that they were done for her by either Mrs. Jane or Mrs. Honour Rush, the mother, or the wife, of the first assistant minister of the Old Church."

With the help of Miss Gulston or Mrs. Rush we can form some idea of a number of houses that otherwise would be mere names. "Church Place" for instance, otherwise known as "Essex House", the "Palace" and "Queen Anne's Laundry", which stood at the corner of Paulton's Street and Church Street, opposite the Rectory, and is described in Henry Kingsley's *The Hillyars and the Burtons*. The Burton family lived in this "very large house called by us indifferently Church Place or Queen Elizabeth's Palace. It had been in reality the palace of the young Earl of Essex" [Parliamentary General and son of Elizabeth's favourite]. One can, moreover, peep into Lady Walpole's grotto and greenhouse, into the World's End tea gardens (at the corner of King's Road and World's End passage), see the last of Shrewsbury House (which the artist mistook for Sir Thomas More's) or be transported to the rural Chelsea of Blackland's Farm, the more rural for the naïvety of the artist's brush, which quaintly details latticed windows and thatched barn, hens and pigs, the thresher with his flail and the farm-hand in rustic smock, milkman's yoke on his shoulders. Blacklands Farm stood on the site of the Duke's of York Headquarters, its cows pastured in the early nineteenth century on what remained of Chelsea Common. "The Family of King George III", the title of the drawing informs us, "stop most mornings here to take milk."

The Gulston picture of another old farmhouse, Hutchins's Farm, which stood on the north side of the King's Road between Arthur Street and Carlyle Square, on the site afterwards called King's Parade, shows the scene of a murder and robbery in 1771, of which Faulkner gives a circumstantial account, quite in the vein of the Newgate Calendar. A desperate gang arrived one night, tied up the maids, robbed and ill-treated Mrs. Hutchins, "One of them struck her so forcibly on the mouth as to loosen a tooth, on which, in the dread of still further violence, she went upstairs with them and gave them sixty-four guineas." They shot one of the menservants, who after they had gone approached Mrs. Hutchins, and saying "How are you, madam, for I am dead," dropped on the floor. Seven men came up for trial; four of them were hanged at Newgate; and as they were Jews, for some time afterwards "a Jew could scarcely pass the streets but he was upbraided with the words 'Hutchins' and 'Chelsea,' a wanton unfairness which Faulkner very properly condemns". The farm was also the final setting of the famous stag-hunt that Faulkner witnessed in 1796 when "the animal swam across the river, from Battersea, and made for Lord Cremorne's grounds; and upon being driven from thence, ran along the waterside as far as the Church and turning up Church Lane at last took refuge in Mrs. Hutchins's barn where he was taken alive." It would be ungrateful to wish these water-colours were more accomplished in execution for they illustrate so much of Chelsea's past, and apart from associations they suggest something of the mellow warmth of brick of vanished mansions, of Dutch-seeming neatness and orderliness, of placid and happy bowers.

The combination of fact and aesthetic feeling is well represented in the nineteenth century by Walter Greaves, who if we leave Whistler out of account, is to be considered as the artist of Chelsea *par excellence*. Greaves (1846–1930) had two objects of adoration; one was Whistler, the other was the Chelsea in which he was born and bred, which he knew the more intimately and from every aspect as a boat-builder's son and habitual waterman.

He spent the whole of his life painting and drawing Chelsea, sometimes after the manner of Whistler, sometimes with that precise and primitive vision so remarkably evidenced in the *Boat Race from Hammersmith Bridge* which he seems to have painted at the age of sixteen. The result is a very large number of splendid works, including Whistlerian nocturnes like *The Balcony* (painted from "the Master's" window in Lindsey Row) which Walter Sickert described in 1911 (the year of Greaves's sensational first one-man show at the Goupil Gallery) as "an august nocturne with a quality of intricate and monumental design that Whistler never reached". It is the "primitive" or *douanier Rousseau* Greaves on the other hand that we see in the early picture of Lombard Street, looking east (1862) where the absolute distinctness of buildings, lamp-posts and a Carlylean figure looking towards Danvers Street attains a certain magic. The same quality appears in his view of the foreshore and houses on the south side of Lombard Street (like the picture previously mentioned now on permanent loan from the Chelsea Society to Crosby Hall). Affection is implicit in the care he has lavished on every brick gable, the tower of the old church, the picturesquely stepped galleries of the "Adam and Eve"; on every crack and stain in the river wall; while boats and barges are rendered with the mastery of their structure we should expect. These, like many later works, are signed "H. & W. Greaves", but though Henry, the brother, did paint, he is as shadowy a figure in the combination as Hubert, the brother of Jan van Eyck, and Walter, there is no doubt was the genius of the two. Lindsey Wharf and the family Landingstage are subjects of some of his best paintings(1). Of Battersea Bridge, he painted several versions—an especially beautiful version with foreground figures was exhibited in London at the Roland, Browse Galleries in 1947. The great frost of 1891 inspired another remarkable series depicting the Frozen Thames and Chelsea in snow. Greaves's *Cremorne Gardens in the Evening* showing the entrance to the theatre, the Stooping Venus fountain, and groups of visitors is fascinating in its union of tawdriness and mystery.

In 1890 "H. & W. Greaves" executed a series of wallpaintings in what was then the Wandsworth Town Hall, reputedly of Chelsea subjects, reported of recent years to be in a state of bad repair. Curious to see them I discovered that the Wandsworth Town Hall is now a warehouse and through the courtesy of the Streatham Engineering Company was able to look at them in the firm's premises, the former "mayor's parlour". It was both mournful and exciting to have a first view of these works which are probably not very widely known and may soon disappear altogether. Painted actually on the wall (frames also are painted round the pictures) they are pitted with numerous holes and gashes in the plaster. They are of the Thames rather than Chelsea in particular: the Pool; Mortlake with a lively crowd watching an American crew rowing on the Boat Race course; the old riverside inn at Battersea, the Red House; but they do include a view of the faintly Oriental "Dancing Platform" at Cremorne with a number of the artist's typical black-coated figures standing round: and if rather cruder in style than his canvases, it conveyed, as a musical hall backcloth might—though on a smaller scale—a sort of shabby glamour.

If we turn to human iconography Chelsea is also well served. Sir Thomas More and his family circle come to life in the famous conversation piece(3) which has also its interesting suggestion of the Tudor interior, the clock, the sideboard with linenfold panelling, the pewter plate and jug by the leaded casement, the books scattered round, the footstool on the rush-covered floor. The image of Sir Thomas himself, as first conceived by Holbein and copied by other hands, has thus been made almost as generally familiar as that of Henry VIII. The National Portrait Gallery half-length is one version that brings the Chancellor intimately before us, the keen reflective gaze, the philosophically clasped hands, the mouth at once earnest, determined and with the capacity of humour.

The National Portrait Gallery, indeed, is full of Chelsea notables. Here is Sir Theodore Turquet de Mayerne, physician and chemist, a native of Geneva, knighted by James I and celebrated as the medical adviser of four kings, Henry IV and Louis XIII of France, James I and Charles I of England. He appears, old, courtly, plump and bearded in the portrait painted by some assistant of Rubens in 1652. Mayerne was then seventy-nine and living at Lindsey House, the old farmhouse belonging to Beaufort House, rebuilt some years after his death in 1655. Sir Theodore must have been interested in art for his friend Edward Norgate, the Herald, refers to his desire "to know the names, nature and property of the several colleurs, of Limning comonly used by those excellent artists of our Nation (which infinitely transcend those of his)". He left to "the poore of Chelsea where I now dwell, the sum of £50". One of his daughters, Elizabeth, wife of Peter de Caumont, Marquis de Cugnac, died during his lifetime, in 1653, and a monument to her memory was put up on the south wall of the chancel in the old church. The Chelsea parish register records that another daughter,

44 Looking along Cheyne Walk from the old church towards Cadogan Pier

From a lithograph of about 1850

45   Cheyne Walk in 1811
From the watercolour by John Varley

46   "Waiting for another fare; the juvenile conveyance between Cadogan Pier,
Chelsea, and Cremorne" (1858)
From the painting by G. W. Brownlow

Adriana, was married there in 1659 to "Armand de Coumond, Lord Marquest of Monpolion".

A portrait painted on copper by an unknown artist suggests the opulent charm and striking appearance of the Duchess of Mazarin(39) (who died in 1699 at the age of fifty-three); while J. Parmentier represents the aged and quizzical features of her friend, St. Evremond, in 1701, at which time he was well over eighty(40). Sir Godfrey Kneller (1711) does justice to the florid countenance of Richard Steele(26) (in his Chelsea period) in one of the Kit-Cat Club portraits acquired by the National Portrait Gallery in 1945. In the painting of Smollett(27), in the year before his death and during his exile at Leghorn, an unknown Italian artist (1770) seems to have caught a look of pain and trouble that clouds and embitters what would otherwise have been a genial face. Among eighteenth-century notables there is the celebrated physician and collector, Dr. Richard Mead (who had a house in Paradise Row), in a portrait coming from the studio of Allan Ramsay (1740); a group of Count Zinzendorf and his Moravians of about the same date: Sir Hans Sloane, tranquil and learned, in S. Slaughter's half-length of 1736. If one wishes to see what Leigh Hunt looked like at the time of his residence at Upper Cheyne Row, there is the sensitive portrait by S. Lawrence (1837) which so well bears out the description given by Carlyle(28).

The unfortunate Dominiceti does not appear in the National Hall of Fame. One would like to have seen the picture which hung in No. 6 Cheyne Walk where "a human subject is extended on a table in a lecture room, the Doctor looks on with a scalpel in his hand; around him stand the allegorical forms of Europe, Asia, Africa and America in postures of veneration and homage; while the Doctor, the chief personage in this awful scene, tramples upon the utensils and nostrums of the Galenical art". This portrait was sold to the son of the Doctor's assistant at an auction "for the relief of his numerous and most clamourous creditors", but its whereabouts, if it still exists, are not known.

The iconography of Thomas Carlyle is a subject in itself. In view of his contempt for art and artists, the number of sittings he accorded must remain a matter of surprise. They were a mysterious rite to be patiently endured, though portraits of him and Tennyson were icons in world-wide demand—as Thomas Woolner discovered when he quitted the Pre-Raphaelite Brotherhood for his brief adventure in Australia. Woolner's sculptured medallion of Carlyle (1855) was one of the principal bases of his fame and fortune in later Victorian days. Each time he sat, the Sage of Chelsea had some crusty remark to make. He expressed surprise at the magnificence of Millais's house ("Has paint done all this, Mr. Millais?"); he denounced the Greek gods to G. F. Watts as characterless beings; to "the creature", Whistler, he gave the order "Fire away"—"When you are fighting a battle or painting a picture, the only thing is to fire away." Yet the artists were not to be deterred, and though the nineteenth-century painter R. Tait is not a Holbein, his picture of Mr. and Mrs. Carlyle in the ground-floor front at Cheyne Row adds to the portraits of Woolner, Millais, Watts and Whistler, a conversation piece which in interest can be compared with Holbein's More Family(3). How frequently also the Carlyles endured the ordeal of photography! and the photographs are perhaps the most interesting of all the Victorian likenesses, both psychologically and in the period character which even the camera subtly appropriates. The character of Carlyle seems grandly and gloomily etched into the photographic plate of 1880(30): in the thin worn features of Jane Welsh Carlyle the camera sums up for us the long affectionate martyrdom of Cheyne Row(29). It is an impressive experience to look into the haunting and haunted eyes of Dante Gabriel Rossetti, so instinct with life and personality in our illustration, one of the several photographs taken by Lewis Carroll at No. 16 Cheyne Walk(38).

In a category apart from the photographic or painted portrait, something more than caricature, though it contains the elements of caricature and humour, a kind of graphic historical narrative, is the series of twenty-three water-colours (now in the Tate Gallery) of the Pre-Raphaelite Brotherhood by Sir Max Beerbohm, in which Rossetti's Chelsea household with its garden, zoo, stunner, and pervading eccentricity is one of the most entertaining pictorial chapters(37). Sir Max has taken certain, though pardonable, liberties with history and chronology in the gathering. John Ruskin, who appears on the right in a scandalised attitude, had ceased to be an intimate of Rossetti by the time the latter settled at Cheyne Walk and did not visit him there. Burne-Jones (extending a flower to a wallaby) and William Morris, declaiming a poem, had also by that time ceased to be intimates in a household by no means in harmony with their tastes. George Meredith, who is seen leaning dreamily on the garden wall was never so much at home and more than one account of his projected stay indicates a brief and uncongenial contact. An account, approved by the novelist, is as follows. Mr. Meredith had, rather irresponsibly, agreed to occupy a couple of rooms in Queen's House. One morning therefore, shortly after Rossetti moved in, Mr. Meredith who was living in Mayfair drove over to Chelsea to inspect his new apartments. "It was", says the unhappy co-tenant, "past noon, Rossetti had not yet risen, though it was an exquisite day. On the breakfast table, on a huge dish, rested five thick slabs of bacon upon which five rigid eggs had slowly bled to death! Presently Rossetti appeared in his dressing-gown with slippers down at heel and devoured the dainty repast like an ogre." This decided Mr. Meredith. He did not even trouble to look at his rooms, but sent in a quarter's rent that afternoon and remained in Mayfair. One has alternatively Rossetti's version, which was that, taking exception to something Meredith said, he threatened to throw a cup of tea in his face. Meredith repeated his remark; Rossetti threw the tea and Meredith left at once: the outcome however is the same. This nevertheless is a minor matter. Swinburne (pulling Whistler's white lock of hair while Watts-Dunton reproves him) is certainly in place, and the model is no doubt intended to represent the redoubtable Fanny Cornforth who was for so long the virtual mistress of Cheyne Walk; though she had her own place of residence in Chelsea, No. 36 Royal Avenue. It was to that address, during the time of his illness that he wrote letters to his "dear Elephant", as he described the amply-proportioned Fanny, chiding her, among other matters, for the disappearance of a cherished pot from

No. 16 Cheyne Walk. In a light-hearted vein also, we have of Whistler as Chelsea knew him, the brilliant sketch by Phil May (p. 135); and on the walls of the Chelsea Arts Club one may find a whole series of caricatures of more recent Chelsea notables in art, including the magnificent presence of Mr. Augustus John.

Old photographs of Chelsea, as well as of its notabilities, are strangely impregnated with the spirit of their period. The late-Victorian Chelsea stands still for us in the photograph of the corner of Lawrence Street and Cheyne Walk, with the Thames Coffee House (uproarious with music-hall advertisements)(47); while village characters in fur caps and velveteens stand with sturdy passivity save where an incautious movement has resolved one into ectoplasm. The trees and railings lean at the historic angles to which the early water-colours have accustomed us in the pre-Embankment photograph of Cheyne Walk(48). The Chelsea Public Library has others of much interest including a fine panorama of roofs and chimneys with the old Battersea Bridge behind still gallantly spanning the stream. Even modern photographs have their tale to tell of vanished charm, like that of Lombard Terrace(49), with the café-restaurant that essayed a continental atmosphere. "The Good Intent" here finds approving mention in the Survey of London. "If it had remained it might have inherited some of the fame of the eighteenth-century coffee-house of 'Don Saltero' which was started close by in Lombard Street. Like its prototype, it had its show of antiquities (if not of curiosities), it provided good fare, and attracted to its benches the celebrities of the neighbourhood." Yet this, the continuous ironwork balcony of intricate cobweb-design, the curved early-nineteenth-century shopfront so typical of its period, in beautiful condition as they appear in the photographic print, vanished a quarter of a century ago.

VII

CHELSEA CHARACTERS

THE unusual people we call "characters" form a category that does not exclude the writer and painter. Turner, Rossetti, Carlyle, Whistler, these indeed were "char, acters", apart from their gifts, with all that the word conveys of the peculiar, idiosyncratic, and amusing (consciously or other, wise) in person and behaviour. Yet there are in addition many not possessing such creative ability who deserve the title even better because they did not write a book or paint a picture and they too have their place in Chelsea history.

An example is Dr. Messenger Monsey, Physician to the Royal Hospital, noted in the eighteenth century, for his wit and learning, rhymes and rudeness. The son of a clergyman in Norfolk, he spent some years at Oxford, studied medicine at Norwich and set up as a country practitioner at Bury St. Edmunds. He seems to have successfully treated Lord Godolphin when the latter was suddenly taken ill on the way to his country estate, and through him was appointed to the Royal Hospital. "He will", says Faulkner, "be remembered for the vivid powers of his mind and the marked peculiarity of his manners", the peculiarity consisting in a license of speech which Dr. Johnson condemned. "He was vehement", we find in Boswell, "against old Dr. Monsey, of Chelsea College, 'as a fellow who swore and talked bawdy'." Yet both Godolphin and Sir Robert Walpole found this no obstacle to liking the "Norfolk Doctor". Walpole wondered why "nobody will beat me at billiards or contradict me but Dr. Monsey?" "They get places," said the Doctor, "and I get a dinner." He lived to be ninety-four, complaining on the morning of his death that he would "lose the game . . . the game of *a hundred* which I have played for very earnestly many years". The length of time he held his office, burying, he remarked, five wishful successors, is perhaps more striking than his wit, but the impression remains (to which a grotesque engraving in Faulkner's

History adds) of an eccentric such as one might find in a Fielding novel.

Another eighteenth-century "character" was Michael Arne, son of the composer Dr. Arne, and a belated alchemist, who built a laboratory at Chelsea in 1767 with a view to discovering the Philosopher's Stone. Having failed and lost his money in this enterprise, he became until his death in 1786 a Bohemian type of musician, composing some music while in prison for debt, though he has a certain distinction also for having conducted at Hamburg in 1772 the first performance of Handel's Messiah to be given in Germany.

Among women "characters" of the eighteenth century must be included two of those "British Amazons" who contrived to serve in the army. One of them was Christiana Davies (1667–1739), an Irishwoman otherwise known as Mother Ross. She enlisted as a dragoon in the Enniskillens under the name of Christopher Welsh without its being discovered (until she was wounded in the body at the battle of Ramillies) that she was not a man. She subsequently acted as a vivandière in Flanders and in 1712 received, for her gallantry, an allowance of a shilling a day from Chelsea Hospital. This warrior had three husbands, all soldiers, the third being a Chelsea Pensioner. She died in Chelsea in 1739 and her grave, over which three volleys were fired at her request, is in the Hospital Burial Ground, though no monument to her has been found.

The similar, chap-book adventures of Hannah Snell are likewise those of a heroine that Defoe might have imagined. Born in Worcester in 1723, she went, we are told, to live in Wapping, when she was seventeen married a Dutch sailor who ill-treated her and left her destitute. In a borrowed suit of man's clothes, she enlisted in an infantry regiment from which she deserted to join the Marines; served in the East Indies in a ship of Admiral Boscawen's fleet and later was wounded at Pondicherry. She received a pension from the Duke of Cumberland and also became a pensioner of the Hospital. She appeared for some time on the stage, singing and going through military exercises, but finally went mad and died in Bedlam in 1792. She too is buried in the Hospital Burial Ground, though, like Mrs. Davies, lacking a monument.

Henry Constantine Jennings, also known as "Dog" Jennings, from his being supposed to possess a sculpture of Alcibiades' dog, was one of Chelsea's numerous collectors and connoisseurs who is described as "an extremely quaint character, short, thin, much bent and singularly dressed"; though at the beginning of his career he had a commission in the guards and long continued daily exercise with a heavy broadsword. He travelled in Italy, developed a taste for collecting, and then for horse-racing in which he lost his fortune. Somehow or other he made a second fortune, lost that also and was for a time imprisoned in Chelms-ford Gaol. He was over sixty when he settled at Lindsey Row in 1792, continuing to spend money on his collection until a third and final debacle consigned him to the King's Bench Prison where he died in 1819 at the age of eighty-eight.

"He came", says Faulkner, "into the world at a time when *virtu* was held in high estimation"—not to speak of betting and the turf: and the "Museum" he accumulated (and lost, like his money, rapidly and completely) was at least as varied as that of Sir Hans Sloane. It included a great many shells, minerals, gems, crystals, cameos, intaglios; stuffed birds and animals; souvenirs of his Italian travels, prints after Raphael and examples of ancient sculpture; some paintings, including a miniature of the Princess Elizabeth said to be by Holbein; and a library of first editions, described by Faulkner as "both classical, and of the entertaining kind".

The passion for objects of art and curiosity appears, indeed, with persistence throughout the story of Chelsea. Distinguished in other respects, Sir Thomas More, Sir Hans Sloane and Dante Gabriel Rossetti may be studied as collectors: and the "characters" of the district, a Jennings, a Don Saltero, repeat the pattern, occasionally with an element of unconscious parody. Though a collector is not necessarily a "character", the length of the list may be noted in passing. It would include Dr. Mead, whose books, pictures, coins and medals and antiquities were sold at his death for some £16,000; the chemist, Charles Hatchett

(1765–1847) who lived at Belle Vue House and wrote a treatise on *The Spikenard of the Ancients*, with his paintings (Salvator Rosa, Gainsborough, Bellini?, George Barrett, R.A.), manu-script and rare printed music (Palestrina, Purcell, Handel, Mozart) and "Mongol Idols" brought by his friend, Professor Pallas, from Tibet; George Aufrere, who took the lease of Walpole House, and there hung the splendid collection of old masters he acquired in France and Italy, which passed to his son-in-law, Lord Yarborough. And then, at Stanley House in the early nineteenth century, there was William Richard Hamilton, the great virtuoso and watch-dog of antiquities who, as Lord Elgin's secretary during the Napoleonic Wars, was able to prevent France from carrying off the Rosetta stone; and shares with Elgin the credit for transporting the Parthenon sculptures to England. It was Hamilton who built the large hall on the east side of Stanley House, and by inserting in it casts from the Parthenon frieze set an example much copied later—for instance in the studio of Lord Leighton. Mme D'Arblay records (1821):

> Luckily the house rented by Mrs. Gregor from William Hamilton, Esq. (who accompanied Lord Elgin into Greece) abounds with interesting specimens in almost every branch of the fine arts. Here are statues, casts from the frieze of the Parthenon, pictures, prints, books and minerals, four pianofortes of different sizes and a excellent harp. All this to study Desdemona (that's me) seriously inclines and the more I study, the more I want to know and see. In short, I am crazy to travel in Greece.

To call this distinguished, efficient, diplomat and scholar a "character" would scarcely be appropriate but an account of collecting in Chelsea brings us finally to a character of characters, Charles Augustus Howell, the "wonderful man" of Whistler's description, to Ford Madox Brown the "Baron Münchausen of the Pre-Raphaelite Movement". As far as residence is concerned, he did not, in a strict sense belong to Chelsea. He lived at North End, Fulham and in Putney for a considerable time and alter-natively at Selsey Bill. On the other hand he was so constantly in Chelsea, and in and out of Whistler's studio and Rossetti's house at No. 16 Cheyne Walk, so closely linked with them in selling their pictures, and furnishing them with amusement and speci/ mens of the "Blue and White" they both delighted in; that he is inseparable from the story of the district and its great personalities. Howell was a collector in the most comprehensive sense of the term. With an immense plausibility and an imagination prolific of fantastic fictions, he was capable of turning any given object into whatever he wished. Whistler one day made a slight sketch of Brompton Oratory to illustrate some point in conversation. That the piece of paper was passed to Howell and not returned was a small matter, disregarded; but the sequel demonstrates his gift of invention. A short while after Whistler was staggered to find the drawing in a Chelsea shopwindow with an attached label: "Michelangelo's original design for St. Peter's, Rome."

He was tireless in collecting Oriental porcelain for his artist friends and others whom they infected with their enthusiasm. One of Rossetti's assistants who lived in the house, Treffry Dunn, tells how Rossetti and Howell tried to outdo each other. Rossetti made off with a rare piece of "Blue" that Howell had discovered and bought, and hid it at Cheyne Walk, intending to produce it later to Howell's confusion: but the latter was not to be tricked, guessed what had happened, found the piece at Cheyne Walk and substituted for it a worthless piece of cracked Delft. Rossetti, taken aback, when he unwrapped the boasted treasure, said, "Confound it! see what the spirits have done."

Indeed, the way in which an object of art would detach itself from its owner and come into Howell's possession by so mysterious and complicated processes that even the original owner eventually doubted whether it had really been his, is the subject of countless anecdotes. There was that beautiful drawing by Rossetti which he and Dunn came on in a sketch/book at Cheyne Walk. "Howell, with an adroitness which was remarkable, shifted it from the book into his own pocket and neither I nor Rossetti ever saw it again." There was the pile of eleven etchings by Whistler, of which, next day, there were only five. "We must have a search," said Howell, "no one could have taken them but me and that of course is impossible."

A comic legend grew round Howell's legerdemain: and one

of the best stories about him, posthumous in every sense, was told by Oscar Wilde. The ghost of Howell, related Wilde, appeared one night to Ellen Terry, and after it had vanished she found that a diamond necklace had gone too.

Chelsea was reputedly the scene of the last sensational episode in the "wonderful man's" career. He was, so it has been generally understood, found in the gutter, one night in 1890, outside a public-house in the district, with his throat badly cut and a ten-shilling piece clenched between his teeth; and died a few days later at the Home Hospital in Fitzroy Square. The present writer, having first accepted this account, which (at once cir-cumstantial and mysterious) seemed too strange to be anything but true, later made some tentative but fruitless enquiries. The records of the Home Hospital did not go so far back: nor had any such event come to the attention of Scotland Yard. Perhaps it had all been somehow hushed up: though it still seemed strange that Whistler or Ellen Terry or Graham Robertson should not have anything to say about it. Ellen Terry, it is true, wrote to Graham Robertson, "Howell is *really* dead *this* time—do go to Christie's and see what turns up." (He had previously shammed being dead and arranged his own sale of his effects): but she makes no remark on the cut throat or ten-shilling piece. Graham Robertson gave a list of items to Whistler who identified many of them. "That was Rossetti's, that's mine, that's Swinburne's . . . You couldn't keep anything from him and you did exactly as he told you. He was really wonderful." But Whistler does not refer to the sinister end. It may be as Mrs. Helen Rossetti Angeli holds, in her Life of Howell (*Pre-Raphaelite Twilight* 1945) that the first written version of Howell's death was that of T. J. Wise in preface to the Swinburne papers. The question arises whether Wise invented it. That eminent bibliophile, was not, as we now know, immune from the temptations of literary invention. He might have thought it poetic justice that a man who told so many tall stories about others should have a final tall story told about him. One would, in that case, be inclined to probe further into Wise's intention. Why the ten-shilling piece? Some kind of symbolism? or was it a picturesque touch at random? The vision of that lean frock-coated figure sprawling under the gas lamps on the King's Road, the sallow visage bloodsmeared, the lantern jaws shut on the little coin of gold remains vivid but without sure foundation.

Another fabulous nineteenth-century character connected with Chelsea was the "last of the dandies", Alfred Guillaume Gabriel, Count d'Orsay, who had a house in Manor Street (rebuilt in 1888), the then "Gothic House", No. 10: the perfect Disraelian nobleman, tall, handsome, well-bred, full of charm, talented as painter, sculptor, and writer, and suitably romantic in his attachment to the brilliant Lady Blessington. One might have anticipated, in his encounter with the Carlyles, the clash of opposites, yet it was precisely this contrast, of which he was quite conscious, that delighted and even flattered Carlyle himself, and elicited the memorable description of the Count's arrival in Cheyne Row:

Chelsea, April 16, 1839. I must tell you of the strangest compliment of all which occurred since I last wrote—the advent of Count d'Orsay. About a fortnight ago, this Phoebus Apollo of dandyism, escorted by poor little Chorley came whirling hither in a chariot that struck all Chelsea into mute amazement with splendour. Chorley's jaw went like the hopper or under-riddle of a pair of fanners, such was his terror on bringing such a splendour into actual contact with such grimness. Nevertheless, we did amazingly well, the Count and I. He is a tall fellow of 6 feet 3, built like a tower, with floods of dark, auburn hair, with adornment unsurpassable on this planet, withal a rather substantial fellow at bottom, by no means without insight without fun and a sort of rough sarcasm rather striking out of such a porcelain figure. He admired the fine epic etc., hoped I would call soon and see Lady Blessington withal.

Finally he went his way, and Chorley with reassumed jaw. Jane laughed for two days at the contrast of my plaid dressing-gown, bilious, iron countenance and this Paphian apparition.

Hardly less effective, though tinged with more visual colour, is Jane Welsh Carlyle's account of the incredible visitor: ". . . the sound of a whirlwind rushed thro' the street, and there stopt with a prancing of steeds and footman thunder at this door, an equipage all resplendent with skye-blue and silver . . . like a piece of the Coronation Procession, from whence emanated Count D'Orsay!" She agreed with her husband that "in the face of all probability he is a devilish clever fellow"; while the servant Helen was reported to have exclaimed, "such a *most* beautiful man and most beautiful carriage".

It was in the sombre 'forties that Count d'Orsay made his second call at Cheyne Row: and with a nice sense of what was due to the period into which he had unaccountably strayed, the "Prince of Dandies" had shed much of his former resplen-dence: "all in black and brown . . . that man understood his trade", approved Mrs. Carlyle, "he had the fine sense to perceive how much better his dress of today sets off his slightly enlarged figure and slightly worn complexion than the humming-bird colours of five years back would have done". Lord Jeffrey was present on this occasion and she noted "How *washed out* the beautiful dandiacal face looked beside that little clever old man's." It was the last intimate glimpse of him though they met again at a dinner party, in 1848, the year of revolutions, that was to give D'Orsay's friend, Louis Napoleon, his opportunity. That D'Orsay should go bankrupt was in the dandiacal tradition; that he should not have lived to take up the post of Director of Fine Arts in Paris which the newly-instated Prince-President offered him in 1852 was an unkindness of fate. In his career of empty and fruitless magnificence he pauses for a moment in Chelsea for our close inspection, a bright butterfly seen through the Venetian blinds of Cheyne Row.

Perhaps the supreme Chelsea "character" is Jane Welsh Carlyle, though her fine, sometimes mockingly concealed intelligence, and the lively expression of her letters make it a question whether she should not be included among the writers. If we speak of her here as a personality it is certainly without disrespect to her pen. With a sudden crackle and thunder of description, Carlyle himself creates their visitors for us, throws his swift flash of light on the townscape, but in the constant domestic awareness of day-to-day events, experienced acutely with a nervous tension that communicates itself, it is she who

47   Lawrence Street: the Thames Coffee House

48   Cheyne Walk and the Embankment
Both from photographs of about 1870

49 Lombard Terrace, the corner of Cheyne Walk and Old Church Street. The café was destroyed in 1939

50 Crosby Hall, moved from Bishopsgate to Chelsea, 1909-10

informs us about the house and its relations with the outside
world, and composes the drama which is so perpetually at the
moment of climax—even if it is only poor Mrs. Leigh Hunt's
request for a spoonful of tea.

> Mrs. Hunt I shall soon be quite terminated with I foresee. She torments
> my life out with borrowing. She actually borrowed one of the brass
> fenders the other day and I had difficulty in getting it out of her hands—
> irons, glasses, tea-cups, silver spoons are in constant requisition—and
> when one sends for them the whole number can never be found. Is it not
> a shame to manage so with *eight guineas* a week to keep house on!

A Scottish Mme Récamier on a horse-hair sofa, she had her
salon, took pleasure in the presence of young, interesting, and
romantic men, like John Sterling or the romantic European
exiles, the scarred soldier of fortune, Garnier, or the Italian Count
de Pepoli "one of the first poets of Italy, the handsomest and
best-mannered of men", commanding them all with witty small-
talk as her husband did with genius. She liked to think that
Sterling "would go through fire and water for me; and if there
were a third worse element would go through that also." She
called him the "Stimabile"—a result of the Italian lessons received
from the Count and Countess Pepoli: while with that leader in
the fight for Italian freedom, Giuseppe Mazzini, she skirted
flirtation.

Servant-trouble was a steady source of interest and crisis. The
crash of plates dropped by a Chelsea native, Sarah Heather
(Sereetha the Peesweep as Jane nicknamed her), sent Carlyle
bounding off in fury to Annandale to fetch a Scotch cook,
returning with one "full of wild Annandale savagery, which
causes the Cockney mind here to pause astonished. Broader
Scotch was never spoken or thought by any mortal in this
metropolitan city." Raked by the combined powers of observation of master and mistress the position of servant at Cheyne
Row cannot have been altogether easy. In spite of her accent,
Anne Cook was quickly replaced by a girl from Fife—Helen
Mitchell ("Kirkcaldy Helen") who made them laugh and was
travelled enough to compare Cheyne Row with the Boompjes in

Rotterdam, but unfortunately got "more and more into the habit of tippling" thus inciting a high-light of description when Jane found her in the kitchen "dead-drunk—spread out like the three legs of Man . . . in the midst of a perfect chaos of dirty dishes and fragments of broken crockery".

She was, she liked to think (for she was not, as Charles Darwin observed, a natural or unselfconscious woman) "demure and devilish", and in her account of those strange ructions that went on at Cheyne Row, she is sarcastically if affectionately aware of the irrationality of her husband's behaviour. Thus she writes to the good friend of both, the second Lady Ashburton. "You have heard, I think, of our troubles in long past years from neighbouring *Cocks!* How I had to rush about to one and another Householder, going down on my knees and tearing my hair (figurately speaking), to obtain the silence of these feathered Demons that broke Mr. C's Sleep with their least croupy crow; when you might have fired a *pistol* at his ear without waking him! Thro' efforts that I still shudder at the recollection of, the neigh-bouring gardens were quite cleared of Cocks; and Mr. C. forgetting all the woe *they* had wrought him has been free latterly to devote his exclusive attention to—*Railway Whistles!!*" She proceeds to describe her horror on hearing loud crowing, the arrival of a fresh Cock just under their bedroom windows. But this time, "Thanks to the prepossession of *Railway Whistles*, Mr. C. never heard the *crowing* under his nose." Her ill-health which matched his—the pains, the sick-headaches, the insomnia—were induced in part by her nervous apprehension of his nervous-ness: of, at night, that moment when thumping and tapping would announce that some irritation of his senses had banished sleep. Yet it was encouraged also by her own in-turned character which subjected her symptoms to a similar exaggeration; and at times, her letters, even when they gossip lightly and discuss trivialities, seem like a prolonged scream.

The evident strain often gives the impression of having some other than its ostensible cause and has led to some theorisation on the sex life of the Carlyles, the matter being considered in the proper, impartial light in an appendix to the Life of Jane Welsh

Carlyle by Laurence and Elizabeth Hanson. Controversy has gone on between those who maintain that Carlyle was impotent, and others who claim that this was not so but that his wife's ill-health prevented normal relations. One piece of evidence put forward by the biographers mentioned above is contained in letters to Sir James Crichton-Browne from Charles G. Fall of Boston, U.S.A., from which it would appear that Mr. Thos. Appleton, Longfellow's brother-in-law, was told by Sir Lyon Playfair that he had been consulted at one time by Mrs. Carlyle for her nerves and had found her a virgin. This it is true is far from direct evidence and roundabout enough to be called hearsay. It may be enough to conclude that they were not sexually well-matched and not unreasonable to suppose that this was in part the cause of the evident neurosis of the household.

This tense psychological drama, that has its moments of laughter and is also sad, has produced, since Froude controversially presented it, in the 1880s a whole succession of books, one effect of which has been to make the Carlyle's Chelsea home one of the most famous houses in the world, and to invest it for ever with the character of its so closely bound and yet disparate inhabitants.

VIII

GROWTH AND CHANGE

THE Embankment made in 1871 was one of the major
alterations of Chelsea's aspect and those who love the
district, still are apt to feel a pang as if at some quite
contemporary inroad of modernity. Any embankment has the
drawback of interposing a barrier between town and river, of
disturbing the organic relation that one feels should exist between
them. The river becomes a spectacle, that, leaning over a wall,
one contemplates with an absence of any feeling of participation
that amounts to a sense of unreality.

It was not so in the old days when the river bank was a picturesque path under stately trees that seemed like the edge of a Dutch
canal and had, as late as the nineteenth century, an atmosphere
of the time of William and Mary: when the balconies and steps
of the old "Adam and Eve" and the "Swan" had an intimacy
with the river that is now only fragmentarily to be found at
Wapping or Greenwich: when the gates and landing-stages of
private houses emphasised the fact that the water was another
main road for the use of Chelsea tenants, and as crowded with
rowboats and private barges as the streets of London with
omnibuses and carriages(11, 13).

The connection and continuity of life on land and water is
pleasantly illustrated in the old prints, for example, in Bowles'
view (1792) of Chelsea Hospital and Ranelagh Rotunda from
the Thames. The gateway is open, invitingly whether viewed
from one side or the other, skiffs are tethered by the stairs; some
wealthy person's barge, with covered deck cabin and six oarsmen
paddles downstream, smaller boats dodge about among the sailing
barges. The architecture gains in effect from this foreground
bustle, the dignified plan of the Hospital becomes lucidly apparent.
The Physic Garden had its barge-house; its relation to the river
is interestingly shown in the engraved plan of the architect,
Edward Oakley (1732) (15), and with decorative elegance in the

plan by John Haynes (1751); the picturesqueness of its water-gate with a background of the famous cedars is conveyed in a lithograph from a water-colour by the nineteenth-century artist James Fuge (who lived for some time at No. 1 Upper Cheyne Row).

There must have been a special pleasure in surveying the water traffic from the pavilions and garden houses, like those of Walpole House as shown in the water-colour drawing in the Guildhall copy of Lyson's *Environs* (reproduced in the Survey of London, Chelsea, Part I); or of Gough House (1720) as visualised in a lithographed illustration to Faulkner's *Chelsea*.

Yet improvement was not to be withstood. The proposal to embank the Thames, made as early as 1839 by Her Majesty's Commissioners of Woods and Forests, offered the advantages of a new main road and of a certain amount of reclaimed land. The work hung fire for many years. The plan approved by Parliament in 1846, which allowed for the construction of an embankment and roadway between Vauxhall and Battersea bridges and of a suspension bridge at Chelsea was halted for lack of funds, road and embankment getting only as far as the western end of Chelsea Hospital gardens. The need for an extra sewer from Cremorne eastwards, and also of a thoroughfare along which to construct it, revived the scheme. The Government, however, refused to disgorge the unexpended balance of something over £38,000 from the amount originally raised. Sir William Tite urged that the Metropolitan Board of Works take over (it was allowed to do so in 1868), the whole undertaking being complete by 1874.

The design of an embankment, a road and a sewer, is not one of the more spectacular opportunities of the town planner and the engineer responsible, Sir James Bazalgette, is not perhaps to be criticised for several aesthetic shortcomings. The stretch of hammer-dressed granite wall is undeniably stern and monotonous and one imagines the old brick-built water-front to have been more cheerful, human and entertaining. The Hospital and Physic Garden have become strangely remote from the river, which was once an integral part of their effect as a composition. Without consciously thinking of town-planning, one may be vaguely aware of an unresolved problem in the double roadways of Cheyne Walk, where the old trees that once marked the river's edge are set somewhat confusedly behind the newer planting of the embankment itself. Many changes were inevitable, among them the disappearance of the ancient Lombard Street and the Arch House which spanned the entrance to it. This building, the history of which goes back to Elizabethan times, formed a curved archway and is thus represented in the water-colour by Thomas Malton in the Chelsea Public Library, though at some time during the Victorian period the arch was converted into the bluntly rectangular opening which appears in photographs taken, prior to demolition, in 1871.

Carlyle was one of those who warmly approved the Embankment as a notable sign of Progress. Faulkner, at an earlier date when the scheme was in the discussion stage, had looked forward to a "handsome terrace" providing a *coup d'œil* that would not then be surpassed in any city of Europe, not even by the celebrated terrace at Cologne". One may nowadays withhold superlatives, but regard it, not without fondness, as an accomplished fact.

The bridges of Chelsea are another aspect of its growth: and the old Battersea Bridge—for a long period, *the* bridge—is, like the unembanked shore, a vivid memory and the cause of lament for a lost and unique landmark. It superseded, in the eighteenth century, the ancient horse-ferry (which figures in the song of Dibdin's waterman) and had been in use since Elizabethan times. "Chelcheyhith" ferry, granted in 1618 by James I to his "dear relations, Thomas, Earl of Lincoln and John Eldred and Thomas Henley, Esquires", changed ownership several times, being promptly sold by James's "dear relations" to William Blake (then owner of Chelsea Park) becoming, Faulkner tells us, the property of Bartholomew Nutt in 1695 (and rated some years later at £8 per annum); later belonging to Sir Walter St. John and passing with the Bolingbroke estate to Earl Spencer who in 1766 obtained leave by Act of Parliament, to build a bridge, at, or near, the ferry, at his own expense.

The Earl, having formed a company to finance it, the bridge was begun and completed in 1771, costing between £15,000 and £20,000, though its wooden structure was an economy as compared with stone. The result was, as paintings, drawings and photographs inform us, remarkably picturesque, in the variety and pleasant irregularities of form which came from the material employed. It was 726 feet in length and 24 feet wide, the spans varying from 15 feet 6 inches to 32 feet. At first the toll of a half-penny for foot passengers and fourpence for a one-horse cart brought no profit, but the increase of population on both sides of the river during the nineteenth-century eventually made it a financial success. Lit by oil-lamps in 1799, by gas lamps from 1824 onwards, it must have been poetically impressive by night. Improvements were made from time to time. Iron rail-ings were introduced at the same time as the gas lamps. A carriage road was made with a raised foot-path on each side and a series of bays where the stroller could stop to admire the view. Faulkner records the interesting fact that in his time each of the fifteen shares which controlled the property entitled each proprietor to vote for the counties of Middlesex and Surrey.

That the bridge was a delight to painters is well known and easy to appreciate; it retains its hold on the affections by Whistler's superb nocturne alone. It gained even a kind of superstitious respect, for the legend grew up (it finds mention in the Life of William De Morgan) that the particular confluence of airs, to be met with half-way across, possessed some strange curative and healthful magic nowhere else existing. On the other hand, Beaver remarks that "the old bridge was utterly detested by 'practical' people, being to them nothing but an eyesore and an encumbrance". Bargees and tug captains would evidently find it difficult to negotiate; while, for its purpose, and in spite of the massiveness of its beams and ties, it was fragile. Severe weather put it out of action for some time as early as 1795. While it aged beautifully it also grew unsteady. The Albert Bridge Company, which bought it in 1873, strengthened the foundations with concrete and threw two spans into one for the convenience of river traffic: but by 1883 it was too unsafe for wheeled traffic and in 1885 was pulled down and replaced by a temporary foot bridge until the new iron bridge was completed in 1887.

Old Chelsea Bridge

There was nothing especially characteristic of the eighteenth century in its appearance. It had the natural and primitive functionalism that might belong to any age; and, for a decade, presented an odd contrast with its Victorian neighbour, the Albert Suspension Bridge of 1873, between Beaufort Street and Battersea's Albert Bridge Road, essentially of its period in style and the decorative importance that ironwork then assumed. The third of Chelsea's Bridges, Chelsea Bridge, linking the eastern side of the borough with Victoria Road and the eastern side of Battersea Park, is a suspension bridge of 1934. "An instructive comparison can be made", says Dr. Pevsner, "between the prolixity of the Victorian construction and the conciseness of the 1934 work of G. Topham Forrest and E. P. Wheeler."

If one considers the history of Chelsea in terms of invasion, it is clear that the main attack on its rural detachment began, as one would expect, in the nineteenth century when the population of London as a whole was increasing so vastly. The population of Chelsea itself is given as 12,000 in 1801, 40,000 in 1841, 88,000 in 1881, and (peak figure) 95,000 in 1901. Why, between 1901 and 1931, it should have decreased again, losing some 36,000 inhabitants, is not at once obvious, though the outward extension of suburbs and the intermediate position of Chelsea between suburb and metropolis may go some way to explain it.

The earlier stages of the development are effectively recorded in surveys and maps. Thus in the "Map of Chelsea", surveyed in the year 1664 by James Hamilton and continued to 1717, "Church Lane" is virtually Chelsea's only street; and apart from the "palaces", riverward, only one or two widely-separated houses break the vista of park, common and arable land. In Richardson's Survey of Chelsea, 1769, Little Chelsea appears on the Fulham Road, Cheyne Walk and Paradise Row are populous, and a series of new buildings begins to define the King's Road, though this was still a private and privileged way. M. Thompson's Map of Chelsea, 1836, the area on both sides of King's Road, a public thoroughfare since 1830, is seen to be rapidly filling in. The old garden tradition persisted in the form of numerous nurseries: the less pleasant tradition of footpad and highwayman, grimly indicated in Thompson's Map by the "Great Bloody Field" adjoining the King's Road, was eradicated by force of bricks and mortar.

To give a connected and coherent view of King's Road, Chelsea and its neighbourhood is impossible, for no coherence exists. It is random in its architecture, genially and cheerfully non-descript, and an account of it is entitled to be random. Try to visualise it from memory and as likely as not you will have a picturesque mental montage in which colourful fruit and flower stalls, antique shops and would-be Parisian restaurants are confused with a few exquisite old houses and the florid front of the Town Hall.

Yet the old houses, No. 211 (Argyll House) and Nos. 213, 215 and 217 are indeed beautiful examples of early eighteenth-century architecture; Nos. 213 and 215 built as a pair in 1720, Argyll House in 1723, and No. 217, at the corner of Glebe Place, about 1750, when Glebe Place was a passage across glebe land (originally to the back of Shrewsbury House). No. 215's survival to the present day is the more welcome because of its celebrated tenants: as the home, for one, of the composer, who according to Wagner expressed the whole of the English character in eight notes (the opening strains of *Rule Britannia*), Dr. Thomas Augustine Arne. Arne (1710–78), apart from this classic contribution to the masque *Alfred* and patriotic music, composed music for the performances at Ranelagh and is further linked with Chelsea as the tutor of Dr. Burney, the Royal Hospital organist. In comparatively recent times No. 215 was the London house of Ellen Terry, who was living there in the 1920s while still indomitably playing old women's parts at the end of her long and illustrious stage career. Mr. James Whitall, who in his book *English Years* has transatlantically idealised the cream panelling, the elegant staircases and fireplaces of the Chelsea house at its best and most typically historic, and sought also for a surviving elegance of life in that setting; was for a time Ellen Terry's neighbour, and describes her, first as a distant distinguished figure, with white face and a mouth of vivid red, surrounded usually by a crowd of female relatives or satellites, later as a charming friend with a fund of Chelsea memories, among them the recollection of Carlyle mounting the stairs at No. 211.

The four old houses, are a single small oasis of the past or, at least, of the eighteenth century in the King's Road. The Pheasantry, No. 152, is an architectural surprise, with its archway adorned by caryatids and quadriga, that speaks of that strange lost cause, the Greek Revival. The Duke of York's Headquarters, formerly the Duke of York's School, for the children of regular soldiers, designed by John Sanders (1801) adds its military plainness to the King's Road approach from the east. Whiteland's House, next to it, a girl's school in 1772 when the Rev. John Jenkins, M.A. lectured on the subject (or presumably related subjects) of "Female Education and Christian Fortitude under Affliction" was rebuilt in 1890. Architecturally, it preserved the linkextinguishers and wroughtiron gate of the original: sentimentally is to be noted for John Ruskin's interest in it when it became a training college for schoolmistresses, and his institution of a MayDay festival, when the goldhawthorn cross designed by Arthur Severn was presented to the chosen

Queen—and, to other girls, many and many a copy of *Sesame and Lilies*.

About 1900 several places of ancient interest disappeared. They included the seventeenth-century farmhouse (Nos. 148 and 150), Box Farm, and the artists' hostelry, the "Six Bells", less famous of old for its architecture than for its garden with its arbours and rockery, its vine-clad walls and mulberry tree, its bowling-green. The medley of nineteenth-century building is completed by the "Italian" style of J. M. Brydon's Town Hall which constitutes, with the same architect's Public Library and Polytechnic in Manresa Road, as much of a point of focus as the length of the King's Road offers: and, at its western end, by the buildings of St. Mark's College, added to Stanley Grove when William Hamilton sold the house to the National Society for the Education of the Poor in 1840, and designed by the revivalist, Blore, "in the Byzantine style".

It is to be remarked, however, that the Georgian idea, if not in all points the style of execution, lingered in the orderly plan of the neighbouring extensions, Chelsea Square, Carlyle Square (so renamed in honour of the great man) and Paulton's Square, roughly speaking between 1830 and 1850. The plutocratic era of the 1870s and 1880s found its distinctive expression along those channels which linked Chelsea with Belgravia; in the "Hans Town" region, including Sloane Street, Cadogan Place, Cadogan Square, Hans Place and the neighbouring streets where there is little to remind one of an earlier age, except for some Georgian houses in Hans Place, and otherwise Victorianism is undiluted. The tall red-brick mansions built by and under the inspiration of Norman Shaw were at all times formidable in their suggestion of wealth and exclusiveness and for a considerable period induced in the critical observers of architecture and social life a feeling of discomfort amounting to aversion, though eventually a "sense of period" came to the rescue and the curious modern mingling of irreverence and respect was nicely summed up in Mr. Osbert Lancaster's pictorial appraisal and his description "Pont Street Dutch".

The flamboyant gifts of Norman Shaw can be studied in

various parts of London, Hampstead and Kensington as well as Chelsea, yet in Chelsea they were exerted to especially brilliant and dominating effect, and Swan House, 1875, though at the time of writing sadly shattered and forlorn after the bombing, was in its way a masterpiece; its projecting first and second floors, its oriels and tall Queen Anne windows giving a new flavour to old architectural motifs.

It forms part of the terrace on either side of the Physic Garden built along the new Embankment in the 1870s, a modern variation on the theme of Cheyne Walk. Swan House occupied the place where a later Swan tavern had carried on the memory of the original. "Old Chelsea residents", said Alfred Beaver in his *Memorials* (1892), could remember its floating pier for steamboat passengers, its arbours and gardens sloping to the river. The new Swan House and its neighbours, though compelled to renounce these amenities, made an impressive addition to this corner of Chelsea. The terrace is substantially Shaw's, including also by him Cheyne House, the Clock House and Nos. 9–11 Chelsea Embankment, though other architects contributed. Godwin providing Nos. 4–6 and G. F. Bodley the River House (No. 3). Altogether Chelsea adds entertainingly to the revivals of the late nineteenth century and the aspirations of the "art nouveau". The architect and designer C. R. Ashbee (1846–1942) who has had a growing number of admirers in recent times was responsible for three distinguished houses on Cheyne Walk (Nos. 37, 38, 39), the Magpye and Stump (1894) retaining the name of the ancient tavern destroyed by fire in 1886: while the new-art, hand-wrought ironwork of the group has its charm for those who can savour the "period" character of even a recent age. Viewed in this spirit No. 35 Glebe Place becomes of special interest as the design of William Morris's architect associate, Philip Webb (1831–1915) and No. 48 Glebe Place as the dwelling (to which he made characteristic improvements) of Charles Rennie Mackintosh (1868–1928), the chief exponent of "art nouveau".

In a similar spirit, one nowadays views the later churches which it was once the custom to dismiss as "imitation Gothic".

Even the destruction of the Markham Square Congregational Church (1860), designed "in the Gothic style" by John Tarring of Bucklersbury, is lamented by the Chelsea Society (Annual Report, 1953) as that of "a landmark which has worked its way into the affections of the community".

An affection of this kind, not proceeding entirely from an aesthetic respect, and at the same time not merely antiquarian, but tender in its regard for a good intention carried out with timid persistence, may be given to the new St. Luke's (1820–4), designed by James Savage in the Perpendicular style. This early product of the "revival of Christian Architecture", neat rather than impressive in its proportions, has a certain cold delicacy not without its appeal. Its principal monument, that of Colonel Henry Cadogan, by Chantrey, has also an agreeable period flavour, with its soldiers of the Peninsular War who grieve over a flag-draped portrait medallion—Colonel Cadogan, son of the Earl, distinguished himself at Talavera and Fuentes d'Onoro, was killed, as the inscription on the sculptured coffin conveys, at the battle of Vittoria, 1813. Among the memorials in the burial ground is that of "William Jones, Esq., aged 83", one of those otherwise unknown persons whom the industry of Faulkner has so entertainingly re-created for us. Mr. Jones, who lived in retirement at No. 10 Manor Street after making a fortune as a wine-merchant, was "eminently skilled in the Hebrew and Greek languages and possessed a happy talent of poetical composition": in addition "painted from nature about fifteen hundred species of butterflies in the most masterly and elegant manner" the paintings being "much admired by the celebrated Fabricius".

A later and more impressive product of nineteenth-century church architectural ideas, especially as far as the interior is concerned, is Holy Trinity in Sloane Street (1888–90), designed by John Dando Sedding (1838–91). The stiff restraint of earlier revival is now enriched and coloured by the influence of Ruskin, whose ardent disciple Sedding became, and the Pre-Raphaelites. It is full of those variegated stones and marbles that Ruskin valued so highly—green marble, red porphyry, onyx and alabaster;

rich in sculptured angels, gilt and bronze; while William Morris's company made the glass for the east window, with forty-eight panels showing saints, apostles and archangels, designed by Burne-Jones. Rich also is the metalwork, for example, the altar rails by Henry Wilson (1864–1934), Sedding's assistant who succeeded to his practice after 1891 and continued work on the church's unfinished detail. In Holy Trinity, Chelsea possesses a remarkable repository of late-Victorian design.

Not a revival but an actual transplantation of past architecture is the Crosby Hall of the international hostel of the British Federation of University Women on Cheyne Walk, brought to Chelsea from Bishopsgate in 1910(50). It was originally part of the house built about 1470 by Sir John Crosby, M.P., alderman, warden of the Grocer's Company, prosperous wool-stapler, and shows in what magnificent state the merchant prince of the fifteenth century lived. It had famous associations also. After the death of Sir John in 1475, his widow parted with it to Richard, Duke of Gloucester. "There", says Sir Thomas More in his *History of Richard III*, "he lodged himself and little by little all folks drew unto him, so that the Protector's court was crowded and King Henry's left desolate." Shakespeare in *Richard III* mentions Crosby House (and, alternatively, Crosby Place) several times.

Some thirty years after Richard left it and under a new dynasty More himself owned, and lived in, the house, though he sold it to his friend, the Italian merchant Antonio Bonvici, at the time when he had decided to settle permanently in Chelsea. Until the Civil War, the hall was the scene of many occasions of splendour under a succession of wealthy Londoners: there followed then the period of its decline. During the war, it was a prison for "malignants". In 1672 it was turned into a Presbyterian chapel. It survived, two years later, the fire which destroyed the rest of the premises, and remained a chapel until 1769. The contempt for "Gothick" then prevailing reduced it to a warehouse, though it was rescued from neglect and decay in the romantic 1830s, its restoration being marked in 1836 by a banquet in the Old English style, presided over by the Lord Mayor. Between 1842 and 1860 it was occupied by a scientific and literary institute. After that, it was turned into a restaurant.

The removal from one place to another of an historic building is not usually regarded with favour: but in this case it cannot be looked on as an act of sentimental vandalism. The Gothic hall was hardly suited to form part of the offices of the Bank of India, which bought the site in 1908 in order to build new premises. The Bank of India deserves credit for the compromise preservation; being at much pains and expense to take down, carefully number and store every component of the fabric, these being handed over to the London County Council. And as, in the circumstances, it had to be moved somewhere, congratulations are to be divided between the L.C.C. and the University and City Association of London for the agreement which caused the Hall to be re-erected in Chelsea, and thus to be linked once again with the memory of Sir Thomas More.

The re-erection was carried out in a precise and discriminating fashion: as may be gathered from the detailed account in the Survey of London: Chelsea II. The original stone windows, doors and fireplace and corbels for roof were set in their proper positions. The fine oriel window and the stone vault with its central boss bearing the helm and crest of Sir John Crosby (a ram trippant, argent, armed and hoofed, or) were put together. The superb fifteenth-century oak roof, stripped of many coats of paint, was refitted. Internally the hall is as More knew it, save that an oak floor replaces the original vanished flooring of Purbeck stone.

It is designed to stand in the same relation to the quadrangle of the University Hostel (the building of which began in 1926) as in Bishopsgate to the rest of the original premises. Strange to think that as recent an addition to Chelsea as Crosby Hall is also the oldest building in it. For the visitor, there is not, perhaps, the same breathtaking fascination that attends the discovery of venerable architecture on its original site. The sense of age has been impalpably disturbed. Materially, however, the building is as dignified and beautiful as ever and could not be more appropriately placed than where Sir Thomas More's own garden was;

and appropriately, too, it contains a replica of Holbein's painting of Sir Thomas and his family, presented by the Chelsea Society in 1950.

Twentieth-century change has not drastically altered the appearance of Chelsea. Industry, as represented by the chimneys of the Lots Road Power Station (1904), remains on its outer edge: commerce has added to its eastern end, Sloane Square, the distinguished architecture of Peter Jones's store (1936). The village character has modified the appearance of houses and flats built in the 1920s and 1935, sometimes with a demure and conscious prettiness of effect. The destruction of Lombard Terrace, a picturesque row of houses on Cheyne Walk, was lamented in 1939(49). The terrace consisted of houses built on the site of the northern part of Arch House, in style belonging to the early nineteenth century and mainly occupied by small shop-keepers. Sir William Orpen referred to it as "this most beautiful corner of Old Chelsea", and the reverse opinion has been expressed of the terrace, Nos. 65–77 Cheyne Walk, put up in its stead in 1929; though having a life not only undistinguished but brief. The houses were destroyed in the air attack of 1941, the waste land left converted into a garden; volunteer effort subse-quently making it each year a Chelsea flower show in miniature. Post-war building is pleasantly exemplified by some new flats, while Chelsea alone among London boroughs has laudably allowed in its building programme for the studio requirements of an artist population. It enjoys also the unusual pleasure, in a severely utilitarian period of that entirely aesthetic amenity, a sculptured fountain—by Gilbert Ledward, R.A., presented to the Borough by the Royal Academy and installed in Sloane Square in 1953. Sloane Square becomes more distinctly than ever the entrance way into an area of London with its own separate tradition in which the arts have a special place.

INDEX

The numerals in heavy type refer to the figure numbers of illustrations.

INDEX

INDEX

INDEX